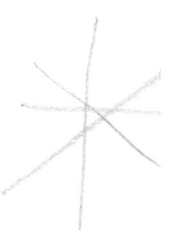

Humanity's future may depend upon strengthening our **agency**.

Multiple interconnected crises call for skilful response on a global scale - but our capacity for **intentional action in our collective best interest** is underdeveloped and increasingly undermined.

This paper opens a dialogue on the contribution of **evidence-based mindfulness training** to individual and collective agency.

Beyond a 'nice to have' wellbeing benefit in the workplace or an alternative to prescription drugs, we'll discuss how cultivating the innate capacity of mindfulness and its essential qualities such as attention regulation, receptivity, meta-cognition, cognitive flexibility, embodiment, emotion regulation and kindness could be foundational in responding to the complex challenges of the 21st Century.

Contents

Please support our work

The Mindfulness Initiative doesn't receive any public funding and in order to retain its neutral and trusted advisory position in the sector cannot generate revenue from competitive products or services. As such, we are entirely dependent on philanthropic gifts for sustaining our work. If you find this discussion paper helpful, please consider making a contribution.

Visit www.themindfulnessinitiative.org/appeal/donate to make a one-time or recurring donation.

Writing: Jamie Bristow & Rosie Bell
Research: Jamie Bristow, Rosie Bell & Dan Nixon

Bristow, J., Bell, R., Nixon, D. (2020). Mindfulness: developing agency in urgent times.
The Mindfulness Initiative. https://www.themindfulnessinitiative.org/agency-in-urgent-times/

About the authors

Jamie Bristow

Jamie Bristow is a leading expert on contemplative practice in public life. Since 2015, he has been Director of the Mindfulness Initiative and clerk to the UK's All-Party Parliamentary Group on Mindfulness. Jamie now works with politicians and other decision-makers around the world to help them make trainable capacities of mind and heart serious considerations of public policy and has supported the introduction of mindfulness courses in over 10 national parliaments. Jamie was formerly Business Development Director for Headspace and has a background in climate change campaign communications, advertising and software development.

Rosie Bell

Rosie Bell is a writer and communications specialist, and frequent collaborator with the Mindfulness Initiative. A recent alumna of the International Public and Political Communications Master's program at Sheffield University, her work is currently focused upon public narratives surrounding the climate movement, and the role of inner capacities in societal change. Alongside training as a mindfulness teacher, Rosie brings a graduate background in philosophy and performance to her creative work with global charities, thought leaders and wellbeing innovators. Her writing has appeared in the Independent, Open Democracy and Mindful magazine.

Dan Nixon

Dan Nixon is a writer and researcher specialising in themes around attention, environmental philosophy and digital culture. He has led projects in these areas for several NGOs, including The Mindfulness Initiative. He currently co-leads the Digital Ego Project for the think tank Perspectiva, inquiring into different perspectives on what it means to grow and flourish in the digital age. Formerly, Dan spent a decade at the Bank of England, where his articles on "mindful economics" and the "crisis of attention" were widely picked up by the mainstream media.

Introduction

Humanity has reached a precipice:[1] our species could have the potential to thrive for countless generations, but the transgression of planetary boundaries[2] and a host of interrelated threats from authoritarianism to runaway technology place even the near future in jeopardy for billions of people. Lessons must be learned and profound collaboration achieved if we are to find a collective path forward within a closing window of opportunity.[3] However, the accelerating complexity of modern life presents us with a crisis of agency, even as our power to cause catastrophic damage gallops ahead.[4] The daunting challenges we face necessitate a step-change in human maturity throughout society[5] - which will however continue to sound like a new-age fantasy without investment in the psychological and cultural resources required to bring it about.[6] This paper explores the case for evidence-based mindfulness training as one such resource.

Even the most optimistic scenarios facing humanity will render life as we know it unrecognisable more quickly than we think, demanding a commensurate upgrade in our human capacities. In particular, exponentially developing technologies will revolutionise almost every industry worldwide within the coming decades. Leading figures in science and technology such as Elon Musk and Stephen Hawking[7] have called for international collaboration on an unprecedented scale to mitigate the consequent risks. In *21 lessons for the 21st Century*, the historian Yuval Noah Harari advises us that "for every dollar and every minute we invest in improving artificial intelligence, it would be wise to invest a dollar and a minute advancing human consciousness... If we are not careful, we will end up with downgraded humans misusing upgraded computers to wreak havoc on themselves and on the world".[8]

Faced with such collective challenges, what might it look like to "advance human consciousness"? This document begins to answer that question by positioning mindfulness, a type of awareness with particular qualities, as one of many natural capacities of mind and heart that can be cultivated through training, and that helpfully shape and colour our conscious experience. However, the body of quantitative evidence for mindfulness-based interventions exists predominantly in the clinical setting. This therapeutic weighting and the siloed nature of scientific disciplines has produced an instrumental and fragmented picture of mindfulness in popular understanding. While acknowledging the advancement in this field, this discussion paper consciously reaches beyond the comfort zone of clinical studies, offering new frameworks for thinking about mindfulness as a *foundational* capacity. Its relevance to many areas of human difficulty attracts the criticism that mindfulness is being peddled as a panacea. But we will ask whether this widespread relevance in fact points toward a fundamental common factor. Through a narrative account of the deeper patterns and mechanics of mindfulness practice, we'll consider it not as a topical cure for society's ills, but a way of being in relationship with the world which supports **agency: our individual and collective capacity for intentional action.**[9]

Each of the three chapters that follow focuses on a dimension of human agency served by mindfulness. For the purposes of explanation these faculties will be examined one by one, but this is not to evoke a shopping list of separate items which happen to receive a boost from training the mind. Our abilities to notice and attend to what is most important, to interpret that information and its implications, and to act well on the basis of that understanding are profoundly interdependent, each creating (and limiting) the conditions for the other. This formulation of agency is in part indebted to Jordan Hall and Daniel Schmachtenberger's threefold model of human sovereignty.[10]

The chapters are arranged as follows:

1 Perceiving: gathering and processing information	2 Understanding: making sense and making decisions	3 Doing: living together in the world
Reclaiming attention	Integrating two modes of mind	Interrupting automatic behaviours and choosing in the moment
Increasing receptivity	Broadening perspective and meta-cognitive awareness	Doing and the paradox of 'being mode'
Building cognitive resilience	Connecting to what's most important	Collaborating better
	Making sense together	

Some clarifications

The mindfulness field elicits accusations of magical thinking when drawing inferences about the effects of individual practice on societal concerns.[11] Let us be clear then: at no point will we claim that mindfulness alone will solve the world's problems. Nor will it render limitless our free will irrespective of the social structures that constrain and condition us. Mindfulness training is not a silver bullet but rather an activator of important capacities within the wider ecosystem of intentional action.[12] These capacities are innate, available and already part of human experience.

This paper cannot do justice to every live debate about mindfulness, and we only hope to advance the discussion by contributing a particular narrative. This account considers the potential fruits of committed on-going mindfulness practice, rather than attempting a robust scientific review of immediate outcomes from eight-week mindfulness courses. For the purposes of this paper, we are agnostic about whether the most common forms of teaching mindfulness are the best way to deliver the benefits we describe or whether further adaptations that more directly develop personal and social agency would be desirable. As explored in our recent *Fieldbook for Mindfulness Innovators*, the sector must always seek a healthy balance between innovation on the one hand, and evidence-building and maintaining teaching standards on the other.[13]

1

Perception: gathering and processing information

> **Just being aware is a powerful response, one that changes everything and opens up new options for growth and for doing.**
> Prof Jon Kabat-Zinn, Full Catastrophe Living (1990)

Paying attention to appropriate information is a foundational condition for agency. But evolution has tuned our drives to favour data relevant to survival objectives in a prehistoric landscape[14] – obtaining the right food, evading threat, finding a mate. The power of these basic drives to distract and transfix has troubled us since the dawn of civilization: for thousands of years, ideas of the good life have revealed a preoccupation with overcoming their magnetism, and liberating attention in the service of 'higher' thought.[15] Conversely this talent for abstract thinking itself supplies another powerful source of distraction from what is taking place around us.

In our current complex world, attending to what is meaningful entails not only evading attentional capture by runaway abstract processing or outdated adaptive drives, but also resisting the potent market forces that manipulate and amplify these drives in ways that derail our individual and collective wellbeing. Mindfulness practice can restore us to some power over our own sphere of attention, enabling us more readily to choose for ourselves the content of our minds and lives, and become more available to each other.

1.1 Reclaiming attention

> **Patterns of attention—what we choose to notice and what we do not—are how we render reality for ourselves**
> Jenny Odell, How to Do Nothing: Resisting the Attention Economy

Writing in the 19th Century, the great pioneer of scientific psychology William James described attention training as "the very root of judgment, character, and will" and "education par excellence", noting that "only those items which I notice shape my mind".[16] While the science of attention has since grown in sophistication, this axiom holds broadly true: our conscious mental states and the whole system of our thoughts, emotions, goals, plans and impulses are assembled and regulated by our capacities of attention.[17] What we pay attention to, and *how* we pay attention to it, shapes our inner world and, over time, our brains and our whole reality.[18]

Agency depends heavily upon the distinction between directing our attention purposefully in line with personal goals, and attending involuntarily to distracting stimuli.[19] The problem of distraction is nothing new, nor is the readiness of market forces to exploit it.[20] Its costs to wellbeing and productivity are increasingly well documented.[21] But in the age of the smartphone, the sheer quantity of stimuli competing to grab attention is unprecedented.

Attention is sacred because it is the foundation of choice

Tristan Harris, Center for Humane Technology co-founder and former design ethicist at Google

A stream of notifications follows us most of the day and night, wherever we go. Digital media markets incentivise the design of apps and devices specifically to snag attention and hold it. As machine learning tightens its grip, this ever-intensifying 'stickiness' entrenches a passive mode of consuming information which is more compulsive than purposeful. Writing from the perspective of experience design, Oxford academic and former Google employee James Williams detects a "deep misalignment" between our personal goals and those of our technologies.[22] If we aren't consciously deciding what to pay attention to moment by moment, then somebody else will hijack our attention and shape our world for us. Consequently, whether it's what to buy, or which opinions to endorse, all of us are swept along daily by agendas that are not our own. While soft power has long engineered our preferences, the destabilising techniques of mass manipulation emerging within and around social media now threaten the aging structures we rely upon to manage large societies. We are already witnessing their corrosive effects upon democracy - not least through the interference of external actors in national elections[23] - and even upon the concept of truth itself.[24]

Mindfulness practice is a particular kind of attention training. Through seemingly simple exercises, practitioners are gradually empowered to reclaim their attention for their own purposes – training the 'muscle' of the mind to notice when it has strayed from its chosen object and to return there. They learn to attend to attention itself, getting to know its habitual patterns and how they may serve or wrongfoot us.[25] Mindfulness training has been shown to protect against proactively distracting stimuli[26] and more broadly to enhance 'executive control'.[27] Often simply referred to as 'self-control', this cornerstone ability helps us to choose what we pay attention to and is essential for intellectual performance. Those who tend to be less mindful have also been found to use technology more passively, whilst those who are typically more mindful are typically more able to "with-stand the temptation to mindlessly browse social media".[28] In a world where global political and economic powers compete to capture, sell or manipulate our attention,[29] training the mind in this way is no mere palliative. Reclaiming attention in the smartphone era is no less than an act of self-defence and emancipation.

Attention is also vulnerable to capture from within. The term 'autopilot' describes our tendency to carry out activities automatically, while we spend about half of our waking life in "stimulus-independent thought" - mind-wandering.[30] The content of the wandering mind is rarely intentional.[31] Rather we are often drawn down habitual paths into rumination, rehearsal and worry. While mind-wandering is itself strongly linked to individual unhappiness, its consequences for the fabric of our relationships may be of greater concern.

Among the greatest human costs of any kind of attention capture is alienation. How many opportunities to demonstrate care and congruence are lost in this way every day? How often do we fail to notice others' distress and fail to respond appropriately? For example, smartphone use has led to endemic problems of absent-presence or 'micro-social fragmentation', wherein people share space but are absent from real-time interpersonal exchanges.[32] In one study, just the presence of a mobile device negatively affected the quality of in-person social interactions[33] and, in another, 70% of respondents reported that smartphone use disrupted their relationships.[34] Social media use speaks to more than attention capture - our search for belonging, meaning and status leaves us vulnerable to what we might call 'emotion capture' too, and researchers describe an 'evolutionary mismatch' between the promises of social media and these actual psycho-social needs.[35] This compounds decades of collapse in community and civic engagement, in part owing to technologies like television that "individualize" leisure time.[36] While online connectivity and peer-to-peer information sharing offer enormous benefit, this need not come at the cost of the real-world bonds that are critical to a healthy social fabric.[37] Mindfulness practice is one way that we can support ourselves to redistribute our attention and our time in ways that better meet our core needs.

Mindfulness alone will not protect us from the attractive power of artificial intelligence that in some senses knows us better than we know ourselves. A much wider public conversation is necessary; so too are policy regulation and other protective protocols. However, as former Google expert on the ethics of human persuasion Tristan Harris notes, "unless we're aware of what's going on in our bodies and minds when we're using these technologies then we've already lost".[38]

1.2 Increasing receptivity

> ❝❞ **The complex system that is the body is a field of ways of knowing, all of which work together ecologically to provide the necessary information.**
> Nora Bateson, film-maker, lecturer and research designer in complex living systems

In cognitive science, the distinction between perception and cognition is becoming increasingly blurred.[39] According to current models the mind holds 'raw' sensory data only briefly, if at all, before imposing existing knowledge automatically: identifying objects and experiences, fitting them to existing cognitive schemas, and telling familiar stories about them.[40] These pattern-matching processes have enormous adaptive benefit, allowing us to impose order upon the mass of information we encounter in each moment and to use predictive models to exercise power within our environment. Shorthand is essential for navigating life. However in a world of rapid change, the accuracy and usefulness of our internal models of reality depend upon receptivity to novel information. Attachment to existing judgements limits the extent to which we notice new information and possibilities, reducing for example our capacity to understand and interact skilfully with others.

While definitions of mindfulness in contemporary psychology vary, most share two key features. First, an element of paying attention or being aware of experiences in the mind, body and external environment as they happen. Then, the particular qualities and attitudes that not only flavour that attention but importantly *shape* it. Besides paying attention on purpose, mindfulness entails awareness that is **open, allowing, curious and kind.**

In this instance to be 'open' is to put aside preconceptions as far as possible, the better to receive experience as it arises rather than imposing knowledge upon it. 'Allowing' refers to non-resistance to current experience. To be curious is to commit and recommit to exploring experience in depth and to sincerely ask what might be taking place beyond existing biases or expectations. Finally, mindful awareness *cares* about its object, whether internal or external, and cultivating this intention develops an "internal climate of friendliness" towards experience.[41] * We may reflect that each of these qualities serves to up-regulate the others, holding wide the 'bandwidth' of perception and supporting an expansive 'shape of mind' that is fundamentally receptive to whatever is arising.**

* Practicing friendliness towards experience is thought to underpin a broader disposition of kindness.[42] Mindfulness teacher-training theory emphasises the importance of offering mindfulness-based programmes in a spirit of compassion and kindness, and of embodying these qualities in order to teach them to participants implicitly. It is also now increasingly common for mindfulness courses to include explicit research-based elements[43] that cultivate heart-qualities like the 'loving-kindness practice' or social and emotional psychoeducation content [44]

** "In mindfulness, we start to see the world as it is, not as we expect it to be, how we want it to be, or what we fear it might become." Mark Williams, Mindfulness: An Eight-Week Plan for Finding Peace in a Frantic World

Box 1: **Mindfulness courses and types of practice**

Although many 'self-help' books and apps are now available, some with an emerging evidence base of their own, most of the research into mindfulness has tested in-person teaching. A typical mindfulness course includes weekly sessions over 6-12 weeks. Participants learn a number of practices to develop different capacities and modes of perception.

An important distinction can be made between practices that develop 'focused awareness' (FA) - the ability to pay attention to one thing at a time - and those that develop 'open monitoring' (OM)[45] - the ability to rest within the flow of life and avoid being overwhelmed by subjective experience. Some practices blend either FA or OM with the cultivation of a specific quality, like kindness or compassion.

Mindfulness courses combine formal practices, informal practice instruction, psycho-education content and the process of 'inquiry', which is the teacher-led exploration of participant experiences to facilitate embodied learning.

Informal practice is the cultivation of moment-to-moment mindfulness throughout life.

The components of mindfulness courses vary depending on their context and desired outcomes, but those that adhere closely to academic evidence tend to share core elements. Most of the 5,000+ peer-reviewed research papers on mindfulness concern the eight-week course Mindfulness-Based Stress Reduction originally developed in the late 1970s by Jon Kabat-Zinn and its many adaptations like Mindfulness-Based Cognitive Therapy (MBCT), Mindfulness-Based Pain Management (MBPM) or Mindfulness-Based Relapse Prevention (MBRP). Some leading pioneers in the field have developed a framework for defining Mindfulness-Based Interventions (MBIs) wherein some fixed structure (the warp) can be interwoven with novel elements depending on its application (the weft).[46] Other courses eschew this approach entirely and have established new curricula from first principles, although most of these are not yet supported by empirical research.

Widening domains of experience

Beyond its implications for the bandwidth of perception, mindfulness might be said to open up new *classes* of relevant information as we negotiate life. Perhaps most significantly, practitioners cultivate greater intimacy with a felt sense of the body,[47] an arena of perception often subordinated within thinking-dominated culture. This rich source of signal is not merely epiphenomenal, but an essential component of good understanding.[48] Notions of 'touching in' and 'staying in touch' take on literal significance, as practitioners restore trust and connection with *sensing* as a legitimate way of knowing the world.

Mindfulness can likewise make more information available to us in relationship, by facilitating better active listening,[49] empathy[50] and 'emotional intelligence' (EI or EQ),[51] which is the ability to perceive, process and regulate emotions.[52] Empathy, broadly defined, names the capacity to pick up on and share the feelings of another. Mindfulness training has been linked with significant increases in empathy in both adults[53] and children.[54] The benefit of mindfulness to self-control may in part result from being able to more clearly identify one's own emotional content,[55] and heightened EI partly explains how mindfulness practice fosters more satisfying relationships[56] and facilitates more constructive management of workplace conflict.[57]

Allowing for novelty

Mindfulness-based interventions enlist the concept of "beginner's mind", emphasising perpetual willingness and capacity to learn, in contrast to being blinded by prior experience.[58] Harvard Professor Ellen Langer, whose study of the subject has extended over 30 years, even defines mindfulness as "consciously looking for what is new and different and questioning preconceived ideas".* Beginner's mind is particularly important when we consider the role of perception as a condition for problem-solving. Solutions to problems we can't yet answer must be allowed to emerge from *what we don't yet know* – but we habitually ignore the natural

* "Being mindful is the simple act of drawing novel distinctions. It leads us to greater sensitivity to context and perspective, and ultimately to greater control over our lives." Ellen Langer, Mindful Learning (2000).

Not everything that is faced can be changed; but nothing can be changed until it is faced.

James Baldwin, writer and activist

implication that in order to be open to solutions, we must first accept *not* knowing. To adopt beginner's mind isn't to do away with our knowledge in an "enough-of-experts" race to the bottom, but simply to galvanise the project of *finding out*. Curiosity is foundational to much-needed epistemic humility.

The prominent mindfulness principle of 'acceptance' or 'allowing' can be misunderstood to place mindfulness at odds with enacting positive change. This difficulty vanishes when acceptance is understood as a functional component rather than an ethical principle of mindfulness. Allowing is practised not because acceptance wholesale is good or desirable, but because it is a *necessary condition for objectives such as present-moment enquiry*. Moreover, the invitation to allow applies largely to what is already happening, or inevitable, and does not entail that we should never act to change our world. Indeed, accepting 'what is (actually happening)' in the present moment is a precondition for appropriate response.[59]

Likewise the invitation to practice 'non-judgemental awareness' attracts criticism from those who misconstrue it as complacency. Judgement is after all an essential aspect of ethical functioning. Mindfulness teaching does not promote non-judgement as an end in itself, however, but emphasises it in the context of practice, where practitioners learn to set aside their stories about what's taking place, in order to return attention to primary data.* (This is not to suggest that it is possible to observe the world 'preconceptually' without ideas and evolutionary tendencies shaping perception to some extent.)

Accordingly, studies have linked mindfulness with reductions in discriminatory behaviour[60] and resistance to bias, including the correspondence bias[61], sunk-cost bias[62] and implicit racial and age-related biases.[63] Some researchers propose that mindfulness courses could helpfully include content on the role of natural cognitive biases in shaping thoughts and actions, which psychologists call 'behavioural insights'.[64] One nascent intervention developed specifically to help Welsh civil servants manage complex decision-making combines mindfulness with inquiry into how emotions and biases predictably distort thinking.[65]

In the context of race-related implicit bias, Professor Rhonda Magee, who developed ColorInsight - a mindfulness-based intervention that supports inclusive and identity-safe classrooms – points to research findings showing that even a short mindfulness exercise may lead to less biased reactions.[66] While our discussion here is focused on openness to novelty, such qualities do not operate in a vacuum. Magee's advocacy of mindfulness and compassion-based practices also encompasses the role of meta-awareness, perspective-taking, presence, emotion regulation and empathy in the development of cultural sensitivity and "the building of the capacity and stamina necessary for cross-racial engagement".[67]

Increased capacity for novelty may contribute to findings that individuals with greater dispositional mindfulness appear to display better 'lateral thinking' and increased creativity – measured by the ability to solve problems that require overcoming habitual responses derived from prior experience.[68] Mindfulness training has also been found to boost practitioners' aptitude for 'divergent thinking', measured by the ability to generate novel ideas and higher-order categories to link groups of disparate stimuli.[69] Recent innovations including Otto Scharmer's Theory U propose that mindful awareness helps groups to set aside implicit assumptions and sense into new possibilities so that their collective learning and strategising is more transformative than cosmetic.[70]

When new information contradicts our beliefs, we can experience unpleasant cognitive dissonance, which can be enough to close the door on challenging ideas.[71] Mindfulness teaching theory emphasises 'turning towards' difficulty and actively investigating distress. This practice cultivates not only self-understanding, but also the ability to gain psychological distance from

* "Often we see the situation (A) and the reaction (C) but are unaware of the interpretation (B)." Mark Williams, The Mindful Way through Depression: Freeing Yourself from Chronic Unhappiness (2007).

states that might otherwise be overwhelming - even becoming "comfortable with discomfort".[72] One study with US Navy Seals found that greater comfort with uncertainty through mindfulness practice supported more effective learning and action.[73]

Again, cultivating such tolerance does not entail ignoring the underlying causes of distress - and without it we may lack the stamina to confront our biggest problems. Many of humanity's current habits are untenable, but the level of cognitive dissonance that this usually produces closes us down en masse to problematic aspects of culture - leading to "system justification".[74]

1.3 Building cognitive resilience

The refusal to feel takes a heavy toll. Not only is there an impoverishment of our emotional and sensory life... but this psychic numbing also impedes our capacity to process and respond to information... depleting the resilience and imagination needed for fresh visions and strategies.

Joanna Macy, eco-philosopher and scholar of general systems theory

Is openness to more information always better? In a hyper-connected, rapidly changing world, the volume of new data available to process can be overwhelming. The futurist Alvin Toffler popularised the terms 'future shock' and 'information overload' in the 1970s, naming the "shattering stress and disorientation" caused by accelerating change and its damaging effect on understanding and decision-making.[75] As early as 1903, sociologist Georg Simmel noted that "swift and continually shifting" stimuli was causing city dwellers to close down emotionally and struggle to respond to new situations.[76]

For centuries in fact, humanity has been grappling with the complexifying consequences of its own progress. Shutting down might then be seen as valid self-defence. But for any narrowing of focus to be helpful, it must be discerning. In the current age we face a deluge of information so fierce that it overwhelms not only our attention, but also our capacity to *control* it: we are increasingly unable to choose what is good for us. A poor digital and media diet, as James Williams notes, creates a new dimension of social inequality where those without the capacity to discern and resist are disenfranchised.[77]

The ability to select and maintain information in the mind requires attention control and also 'working memory', which is the brain system that temporarily stores and manipulates the information necessary for complex cognitive tasks like decision-making, communicating and guiding behaviour.[78] High stress depletes working memory over time, which can lead to more intrusive thoughts, poor mood, psychological disorders and performance errors.[79] Chronic stress also impairs long-term, explicit memory[80] and has a wide range of public health implications.[81] Stress and anxiety can lead to 'perceptual narrowing', meaning that important information in the peripheries goes unseen, both metaphorically and literally.[82]

The reduction of anxiety[83] and stress,[84] along with their physiological markers,[85] are among the most consistent mindfulness research findings over the last 40 years. More recently, mindfulness-based interventions have been found to protect[86] and even enhance working memory,[87] thereby improving 'cognitive resilience', which can be defined as "the ability to maintain or regain cognitive capacities at risk of degradation, depletion, or failure in the face of situational challenges experienced over protracted time periods".[88] In order to be significantly helpful, cognitive resilience need not confront the totality of these 'situational challenges', but only allow an individual sufficient freedom from overwhelm to enact measures that *reduce* the difficulty.* For instance, by choosing a healthier digital and media diet, as Williams suggests.

Mindfulness-based stress reduction is popularly associated with benefits to the busy workplace, and critics commonly denounce what they see as a displacement of responsibility for suffering from the employer to the employee.[89] But acquiring tools for relieving distress does not preclude addressing its structural causes. Stress is an insidious burden on all dimensions of agency, in all areas of life, not least activism and other types of civic engagement.[90] Here therefore, mindfulness practice could contribute to a necessary cognitive foundation for effective and sustainable action and mitigate activist burnout.[91]

Chapter summary

- Attention is a foundational condition for perception, and shapes our world.

- We typically underestimate the many distractions that capture our attention. These can take the form of outdated adaptive drives, the legacy of evolution within us. But they increasingly come from the booming attention economy that manipulates and amplifies these drives, in ways that alienate and overwhelm us, capturing our agency. Mindfulness alone cannot protect us. However, it can strengthen the capacity to attend to what matters.

- Besides reclaiming attention, mindfulness has implications for its 'bandwidth'. Mindfulness training emphasises awareness that is open, allowing, curious and kind; it cultivates an 'internal climate of friendliness' towards experience. Practising these qualities, grounded in a deepening relationship with the body, can radically broaden receptivity – supplying more and better information with which to make sense of the world.

- Likewise aspects of practice such as acceptance and turning towards difficulty can help to maintain openness to important information, including uncomfortable truths from which we might otherwise recoil. Acknowledging what is taking place is a precursor to appropriate response, and openness to change can require tolerance for discomfort.

- Mindfulness practice can help develop the cognitive resilience needed to function effectively in the information age. It can mitigate the harmful effects of stress and enhance working memory - both of which are vital to our ability to retain important information, make independent choices and take appropriate action.

* "The more complicated the world gets and the more intrusive it becomes on our own personal psychological space and privacy, the more important it will be to practice nondoing. We will need it just to protect our sanity and to develop a greater understanding of who we are… It is very likely that meditation will become an absolute necessity in order for us to recognize, understand and counter the stressors of living in an age of ever-accelerating change, and to remind ourselves of what it means to be human. " – Prof Kabat-Zinn, Full Catastrophe Living (1990)

2

Understanding: making sense and making decisions

> **We are drowning in information, while starving for wisdom. The world henceforth will be run by synthesizers, people able to put together the right information at the right time, think critically about it, and make important choices wisely.**
>
> E.O. Wilson, biologist, "father of biodiversity" and two-time Pulitzer winner

Our second dimension of agency concerns the capacity to understand the information available to us; forming knowledge and using it with discernment. To be effective agents we must understand – and yet understanding is beset by fierce problems in today's world. Information overload aside, declining trust in the media[92] and public institutions[93] and an increasingly broken 'information ecology'[94] (the public arena within which ideas are exchanged and new knowledge is tested)[95] undermine individual and collective understanding at precisely the time that we need it to develop.[96] Intensified by social media, increasing cultural polarisation both radically oversimplifies complex issues and entrenches a politics of antagonism that is disastrous for collective problem-solving. At the same time increasing secularism and social fragmentation can contribute to a sense of meaninglessness, and thus to deep existential confusion.

A number of thinkers identify an underlying 'meta-crisis' from which major societal crises stem. The social philosopher Tomas Bjorkman characterises this as "our collective inability to handle the increasing complexity of our world".[97] Writer and transformative educator Zachary Stein gives the meta-crisis four dimensions – of meaning, of sense-making, of governance and of capacity, likening humanity's predicament to navigating with entirely the wrong maps.[98] What most related models of the meta-crisis tend to agree upon is that external, systemic issues to a significant extent manifest *inner* conflicts and incoherence - not least in our understanding of ourselves and of the world. As we shall describe, mindfulness can restore our inner capacity for navigation in a number of ways, and the extent to which it is present in individuals and society has profound implications for understanding. In the seminal text *Full Catastrophe Living* (1990), Professor Jon Kabat-Zinn, the 'founding father' of modern-scientific mindfulness interventions writes, "what we must learn is to bring wise attention to the information that is at our disposal and to contemplate it and discern order and connectedness within it so that we can put it to use in the service of our health and healing, individual, collective, and planetary".[99]

2.1　Integrating two modes of mind

> **Our talent for division, for seeing the parts, is of staggering importance – second only to our capacity to transcend it, in order to see the whole.**
>
> Iain McGilchrist, psychiatrist and writer

The world has always been complex, and the roots of the meta-crisis may arguably be traced to a worldview that does not treat it as such. Systems thinkers such as Nora Bateson locate the fragility of our current historic moment in the unacknowledged interdependency of our systems.[100] Domains such as the environment, economics, food security, public health and wellbeing, and education have been understood and managed as if they were separate – when in fact they are profoundly interconnected. We can no longer afford to operate in national and disciplinary silos, exporting harm to unseen parts of the same systemic whole.[101] At the time of writing, the world is receiving a crash course in systems thinking, in the form of the Covid-19 pandemic. Yet at the level of leadership we seem either unwilling or fundamentally unable to grasp the level of complexity required to adjust our strategies accordingly. This inability to "think in systems"[102] is a symptom of a deeply conditioned world-view, and if we wish to bring about change, we must begin with our way of comprehending the world. In particular, contemporary cognitive science is in the business of revivifying the notion of knowledge – from the flat 'knowing *that*' of propositional beliefs to the fuller dimensionality that includes "embodied, embedded, extended and enacted" cognition.[103]

John Teasdale, who along with Zindel Segal and Mark Williams developed the widely implemented Mindfulness-Based Cognitive Therapy (MBCT), outlines two distinct, mutually over-riding mental subsystems responsible for radically different ways of understanding the world,[104] and proposes that mindfulness practice helps to integrate them. First, *holistic-intuitive* describes a primal mode of understanding tightly coupled to real-time sense data, in which the mind seeks out implicit patterns in the environment and updates working models of reality intuitively. Subjectively spacious, this receptive mode of mind deals in *relatedness* and delivers the world as a coherent whole.

While retaining this ability to assess significance and understand holistically, modern humans - particularly in the West[105] - have come to be dominated by a second way of knowing in which pattern-matching operates upon the basis of abstract, self-contained concepts characterised by the innately *dis*connected and linear structure of logical processing. In this affectively narrow, *verbal-conceptual* mode, the world is apprehended in lifeless pieces; the discrete objects that serve goal-driven problem-solving but also cause us to process in "chunks", oblivious to the whole system in which we act. In his influential book *The Master and His Emissary: The Divided Brain and the Making of the Western World,* Iain McGilchrist explores how these modes of mind have shaped society. Our thinking-planning mode, he proposes, evolved as ancillary to the more primary sensing-intuiting mode, but has increasingly taken over and inhibited it, shaping both our lens on the world and the cultural forces that entrench its dominance.[106]

The practice of mindfulness entails an 'intentional affective shift'.* Mindfulness courses encourage practitioners to notice the tell-tale, constrictive signs of 'driven doing' (goal-focused, verbal-conceptual) mode, and to develop the 'core skill' of downregulating this dominant, instrumental processing in favour of the affective conditions of holistic-intuitive mode. Furthermore Teasdale is careful to emphasise that mindful awareness does not outright reject but rather can include 'higher-order' cognitive processing within a co-reflexive coupling; integrating verbal-conceptual processing into its holistic map. Mindful awareness integrates thinking into an intuitive, embodied experience of the world as complex and alive – a mode of understanding more inclusive of real complexity than the reductive computational model privileged by Western thought in recent centuries.

*Cognitive neuroscience identifies several core affects underpinning mammalian behaviour, which are "emotional feelings... that inform animals how they are faring in the quest to survive." These include states of comfort and hyper-focused "discomfort zones" that drive immediate evasive action. The content of higher-order human cognition can mutually reinforce these base states, such that comfortable feelings may be brought on by comforting thoughts, and vice-versa.[107]

2.2 | Broadening perspective and meta-cognitive awareness

A whole-istic stance should not be confused with a fixed or single world-view: understanding of the whole must find a way to integrate radical plurality. To this end, mindfulness can equip us with greater flexibility in taking new and different perspectives.[108] For example, the effectiveness of mindfulness in many of its health applications hangs upon the capacity to gain perspective on one's own mental processes.[109] In casting difficult experiences as objects of awareness – the origin of the well-known mindfulness phrase "I am not my thoughts" – practitioners avoid becoming absorbed or identified with their content. This is the development of 'meta-cognitive awareness', which is also known as decentering. By becoming less identified with thoughts and interrupting the tendency to believe them as the truth of the situation ("thoughts are not facts"), we may therefore be more able to inquire into them and interrogate their underlying assumptions.

The notion of perspective contains an understanding of partiality. If I describe something as 'my perspective', I already understand that yours may be different and potentially also valid. The possibility of shifting perspective presupposes a wider context in which to move. To put things 'in' perspective is to shift to another position, usually taking a wider angle which includes the previously held partial view. Espousing Robert Kegan's model of human psychological development, social philosopher Jonathan Rowson connects perspective-gaining with individual and social growth: "transformation occurs when we are newly able to step back and reflect on and make decisions about something; i.e. take as object what we were previously subject to".[110]

Perspective is a visual metaphor, and vision is embodied and active. We are not static processors and our model of the world is never complete: we move constantly through our environment along multiple dimensions, testing and adjusting our understanding in a continuous flow.[111] We instinctively move our apparatus when something is unclear, assimilating information from different positions – not in order to decide which single perspective is correct, but to render our understanding of the object less ambiguous and more complete. In much the same way, the ambiguity and complexity of conceptual objects also require us to move our viewpoint: bringing fragments of knowledge into dialogue to enrich understanding.[112]

Participant feedback from mindfulness courses often references an increased ability to gain perspective.[113] For example, among a sample of MBCT participants studied by Kuyken et al (2009)[114] heightened capacity for perspective was a recurrent theme. Numerous studies on mindful leadership suggest that mindfulness helps leaders develop alertness to multiple perspectives.[115] Certain studies *define* mindfulness in terms of the ability to view objects and situations from multiple perspectives, and to shift perspectives depending on context. By contrast, they define a state of mindlessness to be one in which the individual adheres to a single perspective and acts automatically.[116]

Mindfulness practice also develops cognitive flexibility:[117] the mental ability to switch *between* concepts, and to think about multiple concepts simultaneously[118] which is necessary to hold and move between multiple perspectives. Its counterpart, cognitive rigidity, is associated with psychopathologies like depression, anxiety and eating disorders.[119]

2.3 Connecting to what's most important

The times are urgent, let us slow down
Bayo Akomolafe, philosopher and psychologist

The language of spacious awareness should not be taken for an injunction to distance ourselves from the world. Mindfulness is inherently an embodied and grounding practice. As such, it can connect practitioners with greater depths of feeling and intuition. As discussed above, the body supplies an endless stream of subtle signals which are not adverse to thought but rather support our understanding – the nagging feeling in the belly, for example, that tells us we're going along with an action we don't entirely agree with. Reconnecting with this innate, embodied discernment can take time, but with patience and practice it is an invaluable source of insight, strongly associated with the holistic-intuitive mode of mind mentioned in section 2:1.

Among the most crucial functions of this mode of discernment is avoiding ceding our agency to dominant forces, and instead staying connected with what we most value when we make choices. Rebecca Crane, Director of the UK Centre for Mindfulness Research and Practice, observes that mindfulness training enables connection with personally held values such that individuals are "more empowered to make choices that align with these values".[120] The benefit of mindfulness to mental health has been shown to result in part from individuals' improved recognition of what they truly value and find meaningful.[121]

It might seem as if individual values are already held too tightly in our increasingly polarised culture. In the interpersonal space, it may be helpful therefore to distinguish between attachment to ideology and values as guiding principles: the broad motivations that influence the attitudes we hold but aren't identical to them.[123] For instance, the specific content of beliefs and ideologies vary greatly across time and geography, but researchers have identified ten categories of underlying values that are surprisingly consistent across cultures[124] * and which we all are motivated by, to differing degrees and at different times. We might treat these values more like dynamic components of a subtle, embodied navigation system, inseparable from context, moment to moment. When values seem to come into conflict, either internally or externally, slowing down and deeply connecting with the self and the body is time well spent: bringing online an extra mechanism of discernment to enquire which value is most important *now*, as well as the willingness to let go of ideas that contradict deeper priorities.** Thus mindful awareness may not immediately supply answers to our dilemmas, but may fundamentally change the way that we ask what matters most.[125]

Some 'mindfulness-informed' programmes make use of this sensitivity to values in a therapeutic context. Among the most established of these is Acceptance & Commitment Therapy (ACT),[126] which is used for a range of health issues including eating disorders[127] and chronic pain.[128] Its ultimate goal is to help the client develop a life that feels rich and satisfying *according to their own standards*. As such, emphasis is placed on the client working to strengthen their own values, rather than those prescribed by the therapist or anyone else. Evidence shows that ACT can significantly boost clients' ability to behave in values-consistent ways.[129]

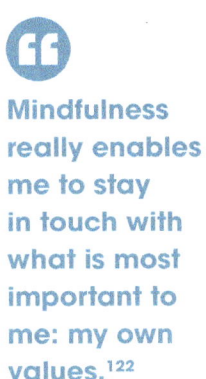

Mindfulness really enables me to stay in touch with what is most important to me: my own values.[122]
Esther Ouwehand, Dutch Member of Parliament and political party leader

---

* Universalism (e.g. understanding, tolerance, protection of nature); Benevolence (enhancement of welfare of people with whom one is in frequent personal contact); Tradition (respect and acceptance of the customs and ideas that traditional culture provides); Conformity (restraint of actions, inclinations and impulses likely to violate norms or harm others); Security (e.g. safety, harmony, and stability of society); Power (e.g. social status and prestige, control over resources); Achievement (personal success according to social standards); hedonism (pleasure for oneself); stimulation (excitement, novelty and challenge); self-direction (independent thought and action). See The Common Cause Handbook.

** Values can be temporarily 'engaged' when brought to mind by certain experiences. Some values also contradict and inhibit each other, so that when one value is temporarily engaged, opposing values tend to be suppressed. Most broadly, 'Intrinsic Values' like affiliation to friends & family, connection with nature and concern for others are inhibited by 'Extrinsic Values' like wealth, material success and concern about image and vice versa.

The relevance of mindfulness to prosociality is the territory of Section 3, but here we might note research findings that when ACT participants are encouraged to pause to reflect by themselves on their deepest aspirations, they almost invariably choose prosocial values (such as 'loving relationships' or 'contributions to a community').[130]*

Another values-oriented programme, Mindfulness-Based Strengths Practice (MBSP), helps participants to identify, prioritise and cultivate particular character strengths in order to lead more fulfilling lives.[131] Values-oriented courses may have potential to be further adapted in line with a growing trend of 'social mindfulness' interventions, which explicitly focus on how mindfulness can support the development of healthier cultures and collective structures.[132]

2.4 Making sense together

> **The cognitive complexity of issues the world faces is more than a single person can process, so it requires collective intelligence**
> Daniel Schmachtenberger, evolutionary philosopher

No adequate account of agency can neglect the importance of the collective. While it may be our cultural habit to focus on the agency of the individual, sociologists maintain that the fundamental unit of humanity is the group.[133] It is in groups and through an inherently social, dialectic process that we develop knowledge and test our understanding.

Moreover, our individual capacity for processing complexity is finite, and the anatomically modern human brain evolved to operate within a relatively simple social and practical environment.[134] Today's big problems have however become many orders too complex for one person, or even a small group, to understand sufficiently or solve. Change is too rapid and the information available to each of us is too limited, our individual 'cognitive styles' too partial and our 'mental bandwidth' too narrow.[135] Collective intelligence theorists propose that only by relieving individuals of the responsibility for building and running a complete picture, and making use of cooperation and collaboration, can groups understand the threats we face with sufficient sophistication and agility.[136] For example, enthusiasm is increasing for political models that radically distribute sense-making and policy development, like single-issue citizens' assemblies[137] or 'conventions'[138] in Europe, mass online participation in South Korea,[139] and digital consensus building[140] and rapid civic responses to the Covid-19 crisis[141] in Taiwan.

Collective intelligence has been studied in the workplace for decades and 'organisational mindfulness' has made a unique contribution particularly in high reliability organisations (HROs) like nuclear power plants and aircraft carriers, where a team's constant alertness, sensitivity to novelty, resilience, flexibility and rapid learning constitute the 'cognitive infrastructure' necessary to avoid catastrophic failures.[142] Meanwhile the concept is becoming *de rigueur* in global business. The Boston Consulting Group (BCG) defines collective intelligence as "a group's ability to perform the wide variety of tasks required to solve complex problems", which "depends on integrating team members' diversity, in terms of cognitive styles and world views". In one study across 31 teams, BCG found that mindfulness training improved collective intelligence as measured by four diverse problem-solving tasks. The authors propose that mindfulness elicits a shift in attention from a narrow, "me-based" focus on the self to a more relational, open, "we-based" focus on others.[143]

Most mindfulness interventions include components that focus on developing interpersonal skills, and this emphasis has increased through adaptations over time. The Mindfulness-Based Stress Reduction (MBSR) curriculum dedicates a week to communication, and some newer

* The prevailing tendency to identify prosocial values is believed to reflect universal human requirements for biological survival, social interaction, and the welfare of groups. That is, individuals and societies are more likely to thrive if people take care of themselves, help each other, and work for the benefit of the group. [144]

interventions like the Search Inside Yourself course developed at Google[145] and 'mental fitness' training developed for the UK Armed Forces[146] give more time to interpersonal and team-focused mindfulness exercises than to silent meditation practice.

Amid the cascading challenges of our 'volatile, uncertain, complex and ambiguous' world, a case must be made for the role of interpersonal mindfulness in political discourse. Indeed where globally significant choices are hammered out at the level of the human individual in high-pressure environments, it is a wonder that greater effort is not already made to understand and mitigate the crippling impact of bias and delusion, brittle identity and unchecked emotional reactivity upon the collective project of good understanding and deciding. While the antagonistic tone of political discourse is meeting increasing scrutiny,[147] the polarising habits of wider society enact the same harmful patterns. From the corridors of power to the darkest corners of the Internet the win-lose, either-or dynamic of polarised political debate is catastrophically inadequate to the complexity of our times. If our true goal is to live together in the world as well as possible, the qualities that constitute mindful awareness can reduce barriers to collaboration. Perspective-taking and active de-centring have profound implications for collective decision-making (perhaps in part explaining why some politicians claim that mindfulness training helps them to "disagree better").[148] If I am not totally identified with my ideas, I may admit your challenge to my stance without personal affront and resist jumping to conclusions about your character. Committed to regulating our own emotions, we may prevent disagreement from escalating into conflict. Motivated by intrinsic values, our mutual commitment to the common good may be prioritised over winning. Open to novelty, we may be more prepared to admit multiple points of view and possible solutions.

A Developmental Lens

The central proposition of this paper is that psychological capacity-building, like mindfulness training, is needed to help people grow to meet urgent societal challenges. Two social theories strongly influence this position, both of which put the proactive development of human maturity and cultivation of cognitive, emotional and cultural resources at the centre of a theory of societal progress.

The concept of **Bildung** can be traced back to C16th England,[149] but was most influential in Germany before becoming foundational to social progress in Nordic countries from the late 1800s.[150] Bildung describes the cultivation of a mature, participatory society founded on the lifelong inner development and education (or originally 'inward form') of the individual. Its advocates propose that nurturing inner growth contributes conditions for the collective to flourish, and become responsible for bringing about necessary social change.[151]

Metamodernism, a much younger concept with discernible roots in integral theory, has yet to emerge fully into mainstream thought. Some use the word simply to describe an era that follows postmodernity, where postmodern critique is seen as having met its limits. Others articulate a distinct new philosophy, or "meaning-making cultural code": an alternative to both modern and postmodern paradigms that corresponds to the digitalised, postindustrial, global age[152] and which, its proponents suggest, can help us to understand ourselves at an appropriate level of complexity.[153] Eschewing an 'either-or' approach to evolving beliefs and ideas, a metamodern stance favours a 'both-and' quantum or meta-position,[154] admitting the inclusion of elements from earlier indigenous, premodern, modern, and postmodern cultural codes. In service of the greater capacity for nuance and complexity their vision calls for, metamodern thinkers place human psychological development at the core of their theory of change. In *The Listening Society* and *Nordic Ideology*, metamodern theorist Hanzi Freinacht lays out a political roadmap that takes a deliberately developmental approach to six interdependent societal domains,[155] evoking "a view of reality in which people are on a long, complex developmental journey towards greater complexity and existential depth".[156]

See Appendix 1 for further reading.

Chapter summary

- While an increasingly complex and sensitive world demands quantum leaps in individual and collective understanding, it is being undermined by factors such as information overload, declining trust in media and public institutions and a deteriorating 'information ecology' (the public commons wherein ideas are exchanged and truth negotiated). Intensified by social media, cultural and political polarisation both radically oversimplifies complex issues and hardens us against each other; disastrous for collective problem-solving.

- This chapter explored two distinct ways of understanding the world – one in which the mind seeks out patterns in the environment and intuitively relates them to deliver the world as a coherent, dynamic "whole", and another in which we process the world into "chunks", in service of discrete, goal-driven problem-solving.

- Dominance of this second mode in Western culture had led us to pursue societal goals in mutually inconsiderate siloes, ignoring their interdependency with increasingly catastrophic results.

- Mindfulness can help us better integrate these two modes of understanding, helping practitioners to bring online a whole-istic worldview more supportive of effective agency amid dynamic complexity.

- The kind of understanding that can underpin collective agency at the scale humanity now requires must integrate radical plurality. Mindfulness equips us with flexibility to take new, wider, and different perspectives, inviting us to loosen identity with our individual thoughts, and view them as mental events ('de-centering').

- Mindfulness grounds understanding in the body, an invaluable source of insight and access to deepest values. Some mindfulness courses explicitly support participants to identify and orient towards what is most important to them.

- Today's big problems are many orders too complex for individuals to solve, and we need to find ways to distribute understanding and discern collectively. Mindfulness practice can support the cognitive infrastructure required to handle complexity in teams and can reduce barriers to collaboration. Training methods are evolving to increase focus on the interpersonal.

- The qualities that constitute interpersonal mindfulness can support better collaboration in political discourse.

3

Doing: living together in the world

A third dimension of agency must prevail for us to carry out our well-founded intentions – to act effectively. In this final chapter, we hope to demonstrate that the practice of mindfulness facilitates intentional doing, cementing its role as a key component of agency. While in some quarters mindfulness teaching invites simplistic caricatures that privilege 'being' over 'doing', foundational teaching theory describes a much more nuanced relationship between the two, placing considerable emphasis upon healthy and skilful behaviour.[157]

In both individual and collective arenas, intentional action is subject to interference from inner and outer forces. Throughout life, our aspirations must constantly do battle with involuntary impulses and entrenched habits. We need only attempt to turn against the stream of prevailing behavioural patterns to discover how strong are the personal and cultural currents that keep momentum behind the status quo, contributing to the 'gap' that psychologists describe between our ethical intentions and actual behaviour.[158] Interpersonally, emotional systems and identities interact in unpredictable and often problematic ways that can derail collective intentions.

These forces too have acquired a digital dimension. While certain applications of digital technology may help us to change behaviour and act more effectively individually and in groups, many more make this harder, whether by distractions tuned to stimulate ancient threat or reward systems in the brain, or by exacerbating the cultural fragmentation and reactivity that lead to conflict.[159]

Evidence follows as to how mindfulness practice helps people to step out of undesirable behavioural patterns, supporting them to act consciously and creatively more of the time, rather than reacting blindly through habit or instinct.[160] We'll also reflect upon the positive contribution of mindfulness to relationships, prosocial action, and collaboration.

3.1 | Interrupting automatic behaviours and choosing in the moment

> **Between stimulus and response there is a space. In that space is our power to choose our response. In our response lies our growth and our freedom.**
> Viktor Frankl, paraphrased by Stephen Covey

Many clinical applications of mindfulness training address problems related to automatic behaviour. For example, mindfulness has been shown to interrupt patterns of habitual ruminative thinking that can lead to depressive relapse.[161] Promising studies associate mindfulness with a reduction in automatic eating,[162] as well as automatic drinking behaviours among individuals with alcohol problems.[163] While all such relief can only be welcome, it may be that this siloed medical approach has somewhat obscured an important, foundational function of mindfulness: namely that *upstream* of automatic behaviours, mindfulness practice supports intentional action.[164] In committing to mindfulness, we undertake to know what we are doing when we are doing it, replacing automatic behaviour with skill and consideration. To live mindfully is to live, more of the time, *on purpose*.

Among the most salient learning points that participants commonly take from a mindfulness course is the distinction between reacting and responding to experience.[165] Reactivity is associated with 'autopilot' and commonly refers to the triggering of problematic impulses or habits, especially where a mild stimulus produces prolonged or intense negative emotions[166] or ruminative thinking patterns.[167] Reactivity isn't only the impulse to bite back, but also for example to 'fix' things before we understand them, which can undermine effective action. The reduction of reactivity is one of the clearest mechanisms that underpin the clinical effects of mindfulness-based interventions,[168] and several studies link trait mindfulness to lower levels of reactivity[169] and impulsivity.[170] Responsiveness, by contrast, is an attentive and creative process that is more sensitive to the specific situation. In everyday life, practitioners become familiar with the 'mindful pause': interrupting the flow of action to check in with inner and outer stimuli and restoring fuller awareness to the ecosystem of intention, action, environment and potential consequence. Over time, they can learn to detect habits of automatic thinking and behaviour, and to acknowledge impulses without being obliged to react.

Reducing reactivity need not prohibit spontaneity. With practice, spontaneous impulse can be integrated within open mindful awareness, interrupted only where it manifests as unskilful or misaligned with intentions. As such, dispositional mindfulness has been associated with an increased likelihood of pleasurable and high-performance flow experiences in creative or performance tasks,[171] while conversely it has been linked with reduced 'dark flow' in the context of problem gambling.[172]

The consequences of reactivity for individuals and communities can be enormous. Antisocial actions – a harsh comment, a slam of the door – often arise automatically in reaction to stress or perceived threat. Viewed separately, such moments may seem fleeting and inconsequential. Yet few occur in isolation: it is easy to see how each transfers stress to another person, generating further reactivity in turn. At the level of our social fabric, the sum of 'low-level harm' that ripples out into the world through reactive behaviour may be very significant. Beyond everyday exchanges, reactivity contributes to many more seriously violent or otherwise harmful acts.

Self-regulation can be defined as the dynamic process by which people manage competing demands on their time and resources as they strive to achieve desired outcomes whilst preventing or avoiding undesired outcomes.[173] It is the foundation of good choice-making. Mindfulness practice has been found to bolster crucial aspects of self-regulation, particularly emotional regulation, and evidence points to an improved likelihood of making healthy choices.[174]

3.2   Doing and the paradox of 'being mode'

❝ Presence of mind is often clouded by all kinds of pressures, desires and anxieties. Mindfulness helps dispel those clouds, so that people can see clearly and act incisively.
Guy Claxton, Professor of Learning Sciences and educational psychology author

In supplanting autopilot, mindfulness restores the possibility of intentional action. We may begin to see then that misinterpretations of mindfulness as essentially passive are incomplete; indeed such criticism usually arises when concepts from theory and research are taken out of context rather than understood within a wider matrix of principles and practices. One such concept is that of 'being mode':[175] a practised state of non-striving. On the face of it such a practice may seem hostile to action. But as Segal, Williams

& Teasdale emphasise in *Mindfulness-Based Cognitive Therapy for Depression*, "*Being mode is not a special state in which all activity has to stop.* Doing and being are both modes of mind that can accompany any activity or lack of activity." The authors don't contrast being mode with doing per se but with doing of a particular flavour, which they call 'driven-doing': default striving to close the gap between how things are and how we want them to be, when that approach is unfruitful or even detrimental.*

Being mode facilitates the greater engagement that underpins *purposeful* action. Far from encouraging docility, anecdotal accounts credit committed mindfulness practice with an increased level of responsiveness that can be life-changing.[176]

Just *stopping* doesn't sound much like positive action until we realise that we've been going in the wrong direction. Misaligned actions can effectively cancel out each other's effect. What matters then is not the total magnitude of actions, but instead their level of congruence regarding a particular aim. Learning to pause, to be still and discern the most appropriate next step can actually enable or speed up the overall progress towards a goal.

Researching the direct link between mindfulness and real-world action brings methodological challenges, however. Furthermore, it is far from certain that mindfulness as it is most commonly taught, with clinical influences and a primary focus on the individual, will be sufficient to elicit direct action upon pressing societal issues. Members of the Mindfulness and Social Change Network, especially proponents of 'social mindfulness' who include inquiry into cultural and relational context in their interventions, suggest that training courses need to evolve in order to do so.[177] Nonetheless, early studies have observed that even without explicit ethical components, existing mindfulness courses made prosocial behaviour more likely immediately after training and promoted "compassionate helping" whilst reducing prejudice and retaliation.[178] Studies have found that participants who had just completed a mindfulness training course were significantly more likely than a control group to offer help to someone in need,[179] a result that authors attribute to increased intention to alleviate discomfort but which could also indicate overcoming behaviour relating to automaticity[180] such as the 'Bystander Effect'.[181] Some studies have also linked high mindfulness scores with more ethical decision-making,[182] lower levels of cheating in a laboratory task[183] and more environmentally responsible behaviour.[184]

A mindfulness course generally combines mindfulness practices and mindful inquiry into participant experience with psychoeducation content specific to the primary intended outcome, such as reduced stress (MBSR) or addictive behaviour (MBRP). If, for instance, civic engagement or consideration of global challenges is the primary desired outcome, then the psychoeducation component might be tailored accordingly (although with great care and deep literacy in theory and practice of existing programmes; see *Fieldbook for Mindfulness Innovators*)[185] and grounded in existing approaches from the wider psychology literature on ethics, values, virtues and character strengths.[186] For instance, one such programme that includes explicit ethical components was found to increase 'personal growth' and the likelihood of charitable giving, whilst maintaining roughly equivalent stress reduction to MBSR.[187] Adaptations such as these may help to more directly encourage sustainable behaviour or actions that address social inequalities.[188]**

* For example, one is likely to feel frustrated or even angry when interrupted whilst trying to complete a routine chore as quickly as possible in order to get it out of the way. But if we accept that the chore has to be done and approach the activity in being mode, then the activity exists for its own sake in its own time and an interruption is treated as something that presents a choice about what to do at that moment rather than as a source of irritation. See Segal, Williams & Teasdale. Mindfulness-Based Cognitive Therapy for Depression (2013) page 74.

** In most contexts there are limitations on what can ethically be included in transformative interventions for them to satisfy the requirement of relative 'liberal neutrality', particularly where public money is used. In a paper titled 'The Ethics and Politics of Mindfulness-Based Interventions (MBIs)', public health ethics researcher Andreas T. Schmidt defines this as the concern that: "...public policies should not aim to promote particular conceptions of the good and in justifying institutions and public policy we should only rely on reasons acceptable to people with differing (reasonable) conceptions of the good". Schmidt goes on to say that for interventions like mindfulness to be accepted in society, it's vital they can theoretically support us to "pursue conceptions of the good—more or less—whatever those conceptions are". As such, mindfulness courses could equip and support people to ask big questions about themselves and their place in the world, but in most applications, they cannot jump in with any answers.[189]

Mindfulness and action on the climate crisis

Too often, arguments for climate action ignore the inner dimension of the problem. The need for a fundamental shift in mindset (values and worldviews) has been 'vastly neglected' in existing research, according to sustainability scholars.[190]

Mindset shift represents a 'deep' leverage point for change – harder than others to influence, but of profoundly greater potential impact.[191] Experts highlight the potential of mindfulness practice to support such a shift.[192]

Research suggests that dispositional mindfulness and associated training can:

- help individuals come into contact with their actual experience of, and emotions towards, the natural world. Since shifting mindsets requires engaging both head and heart, the importance of establishing this connection cannot be overstated.

- support more holistic ways of thinking. As British Green Party MP Caroline Lucas suggests, mindfulness can increase "not only people's exposure to nature, but their immersion in it: their sense of not being separate from it".[193] Awareness of the self as embedded in natural systems has dramatic implications, encouraging individuals to model the consequences of their choices and acknowledge themselves as agents of change.

- support the cultivation of capacities such as cognitive flexibility, problem-solving, multiple perspective-taking and the overcoming of cognitive/emotional biases (such cognitive shortcuts are particularly unhelpful in processing complex, highly uncertain and slow-moving problems like the climate crisis).[194]

Although the science is still nascent, promising evidence correlates mindfulness with sustainable consumption and behaviour[195] as well as related factors such as enhanced subjective well-being, reduced automaticity, activation of (intrinsic/ non-materialistic) core values, greater nature connection, improved pro-sociality, openness to new experiences and responsiveness to events.[196]

3.3 | Collaborating better

> We can take back our ability to create strong networks of care and well-being that are resilient to systemic failure. In fact, these networks of distributed agency among sovereign individuals who actually care for each other, is the core of human evolutionary success.

Bonnita Roy, philosopher and author

While the belief that human beings are governed by self-interest has long prevailed in Western thought, evidence is mounting that our success through the millennia owes at least as much to our natural tendencies for generosity, kindness, care and compassion.[197] At very least it seems we are due a rebalancing of our self-concept: an excessively negative view of ourselves and others stymies collaboration and active citizenship, as well as tainting the public imaginary. Eastern philosophies have long acknowledged both light and shade in our character, proposing that we can tip the balance in favour of the former through practises that specifically cultivate kindness and compassion. Modern science is now starting to support these claims[198] and phrases like 'training the heart' or 'practising heartfulness' are finding a place amongst the popular rhetoric of mind-training.

This shift in emphasis cannot come quickly enough. Action of sufficient magnitude to address the converging crises we now face must be collective, but as Indra Adnan notes in *The Politics of Waking Up*, currently "even people who broadly agree cannot collaborate successfully".[199] Adnan, a writer, psychosocial therapist and political entrepreneur, proposes that while the Internet has left us more socially fragmented and politically polarised, a dominant conception of human beings as primarily economic units is also undermining our shared agency. As a result it has perhaps never been harder to provide effective leadership or galvanise collective response. Again we must emphasize that the systemic issues at play here won't be solved just through psychological capacity-building like mindfulness and compassion training. However it must by now be clear that we require all the help that we can give ourselves to pull together more effectively.

Perhaps unsurprisingly, qualitative feedback from participants in mindfulness-based programmes points strongly to positive effects upon interpersonal relationships.[200] Participants in one clinical study, which identified improved relationships as one of four major themes, described greater emotional closeness with friends and family, better communication, relating more constructively, reduced anger and increased empathy.[201] Preliminary studies have directly explored the impact of training upon interpersonal relating,[202] leadership skills,[203] interpersonal forgiveness,[204] discrimination,[205] retaliation,[206] and conflict resolution.[207]

Previous chapters have considered the contribution of mindfulness to emotional intelligence, empathy and listening, cognitive flexibility and perspective-taking, values-awareness, emotion regulation and reduced reactivity - all mutually beneficial qualities that interact to support better social bonds. Also important in this relational ecosystem are the effects of mindfulness practices on anger and aggression, and their role in cultivating compassion.

Anger and aggression

Anger is part of a normal emotional spectrum and may be productive in certain circumstances.[208] Philosophers dating back to Aristotle have considered righteous indignation a moral virtue.[209] However, aggressive or impulsive expression of anger can also be highly destructive for individuals and groups,[210] leading to feelings such as fear and blame, thoughts of revenge, and increased incivility[211] that can sink collective agency.

Studies link dispositional mindfulness to lower aggression,[212] anger[213] and workplace hostility,[214] particularly through reduced rumination[215] and use of dysfunctional regulation strategies.[216] Appropriate anger regulation likely contributes significantly to the improved relationship satisfaction associated with mindfulness training.[217] There is also evidence that mindfulness buffers against the "physiological effects of relationship conflict" such as raised cortisol and cardiovascular activity.[218] Initial trials of mindfulness interventions have found reductions in anger across diverse populations including cardiovascular patients,[219] schizophrenic patients,[220] those with autism[221] or intellectual disability,[222] psychotherapists in training,[223] police officers[224] and the prison population.[225]

Empathy and compassion

Compassion takes the understanding and resonance of empathy further toward action through the ability to tolerate one's own emotional reaction and a motivation to relieve another's suffering. Empirically, empathy and compassion are linked to an increase in helping and pro-social behaviour, deeper feelings of intimacy, lower aggressiveness and reduced antisocial behaviour.[226] Both are trainable capacities that could be vital to our ability to connect with each other and relate productively within teams and across divides.[227]

By, for example, regulating attention, reducing automatic judgement, encouraging perspective-taking and engaging a receptive attitude towards others, mindfulness training promotes the conditions necessary for both empathy and compassion, and a number of studies have demonstrated correlation and causation.[228] There is evidence that mindfulness training helps participants to cope with empathic distress, or rather tips their responses towards empathic concern instead of distress, thereby enabling compassionate behaviour.[229]

The role of explicit prosocial components in mindfulness courses

Many mindfulness interventions tested for their impact on prosocial affect* have included some explicit kindness, compassion or 'social and emotional learning' elements. A recent meta-analysis showed that effects were comparable regardless of whether or not courses included explicit prosocial content, but it is also widely suggested that whilst mindful awareness provides a necessary foundation it is only the first step towards also training the heart.[230] One large and unusually robust trial that directly compared three-month training modules in 'presence' (attention & embodiment), 'affect' (care, compassion & emotion regulation) and 'perspective' (metacognition & perspective-taking) found that the affect module was required for broad changes in prosocial qualities[231] and provides evidence that disambiguating these different types of mind-heart cultivation might help to develop more targeted interventions. A burgeoning field of innovation and inquiry is exploring mindfulness courses that have explicit compassion components like Mindfulness-Based Compassionate Living[232] and 'mindfulness-informed' compassion-focussed trainings such as Compassion-Focussed Therapy[233] and Mindful Self-Compassion.[234] [235] Again, we are agnostic as to whether standard mindfulness courses (such as MBSR and MBCT) sufficiently develop prosocial affect relative to those programmes that make this an explicit aim and priority. We simply make a case here for training the heart and mind through practices that take mindful awareness as a foundational proposition.

* Affect is a psychological term for any experience of feeling or emotion

Human beings have progressively widened the circle of empathy and compassion that we feel for others,[236] from family and tribes to ever more distant and different humans and animals.[237] To maintain this trend amid the fragmenting and alienating disruptions to which our societies are subject, it is vital that we more consciously develop our capacity to see and stay open to others when they are in distress.[238] We can as yet only imagine what depth of personal resource will be required of us to bear witness and respond to future crises. There is every imperative therefore to cultivate these capacities in more stable times - and mindfulness training can be a robust foundation.

Chapter summary

- A third dimension of agency must prevail for us to act, intentionally and effectively. Despite a common misconception of mindfulness as somehow passive, practice in fact helps to restore intention as a driver of action – allowing us to know what we are doing, when we are doing it. Reduction in automatic behaviour and harmful reactivity are central to the efficacy of mindfulness training.

- We know that mindfulness practice helps individuals to act consciously and creatively more of the time. In the context of human survival on a planetary scale, however, effective action has to be collective. While in the past Western belief has held that human beings are governed by self-interest, we can tip the scales in favour of collaboration through practices that specifically cultivate innate, prosocial qualities.

- Evidence shows that mindfulness practices can decrease impulsivity, anger and aggression. Coupled with practices that cultivate compassion, this can help to reduce some of the blocks that inhibit collaborative working.

- Mindfulness training has also been shown to increase the empathy and compassion we feel for those around us, enabling more compassionate behaviour and responses to those in distress.

Closing reflections

Our proposal then is both modest *and* ambitious. We say that the natural human capacity of mindfulness can support our collective efforts to figure out what to do, based on an adequate understanding of appropriate information, and do it. It's modest because this basic formulation of agency is an assumption on which we already operate. It's ambitious however because as we have seen, owing to an array of confounding forces both within the human mind and body and our cultural environment, this is harder to achieve than we may know.

As the clock ticks down on irreversible climate change and multiple interconnected crises, activating individual and collective agency is not a lifestyle extra - it is a matter of survival. The challenges ahead are grave but crisis can precipitate intelligent and adaptive development. And at this time, anyone with a serious care for our future would do well to look beyond customary perspectives and problem-solving strategies that may be an ill fit for complexity. Recognised as an innate, foundational capacity, mindfulness has the potential to become both a core part of a collective vision for society, and a way to help make that vision a reality. That such a potentially powerful instrument of transformation has already gained such appeal in governments, workplaces and communities[239] is unusual if not unheard of - a strong case for investing energy in fulfilling its potential.

Every available means will be required to steer humanity away from its precipice. But whether or not global society is fortunate enough to escape worst-case scenarios, accelerating change will continue to present us with existential questions. As the 'fourth industrial revolution' advances, bringing with it increasing automation and escalating AI, it will be ever more necessary to retell our stories of purpose and value around qualities that are innately human. Indeed it has been suggested that we are entering the age of *humanics* rather than robotics: "an age that integrates our human and technological capacities to meet the global challenge of our time."[240]

How will we rise above the tensions brought about by radical change, to live into this future well, and with meaning? From all quarters we are called urgently to a better understanding of ourselves, each other and our role in shaping the world. Tools are available, if we wish, to begin at once: to reclaim and reorient attention towards what matters, reflect more wisely, and act from a place of collective purpose. Great possibility waits very close to where we are, and in developing mindfulness we mobilise a powerful foundational capacity for agency in urgent times.

ALSO AVAILABLE NOW:

Responding to 'Mindfulness: Developing Agency in Urgent Times' is a compilation of essays by researchers, innovators and thinkers that critically engage with the topics outlined in the Mindfulness Initiative's *Mindfulness: Developing Agency in Urgent Times* publication.

> **This collection is a welcome example of the conversations that we need more of, and in ever greater depth across a broad range of interfaces within society**
> Jon Kabat-Zinn

Mindfulness: Developing Agency in Urgent Times has been described as a landmark publication for the field, and explores the potential for mindfulness to underpin intentional action (or 'agency') in addressing complex societal and global challenges.

In order to continue this important conversation, we asked researchers, innovators and thinkers to submit a response to the document. We then invited a selection of contributors to develop their thoughts into short essays, which we have now published in a collection.

Responding to 'Mindfulness: Developing Agency in Urgent Times is composed of 11 essays, each of which discusses different topics relating to the MI's recent publication, such as how mindfulness training might need to evolve to better meet societal challenges, additional ways it might be vital for improving our relationships with technology, or how the mindfulness sector should focus on community and decolonisation to unlock its transformative potential.

Download here: bit.ly/respondingtomindfulness

Acknowledgements

Grateful thanks to the funders of the Mindfulness Initiative for their faith and support. Thank you to the Lostand Foundation, Mindful Trust and Sankalpa.

Our deep appreciation to the web of devoted change-makers, researchers, social philosophers and many other visionary thinkers to whose ideas we are indebted in telling this story, and in particular to Indra Adnan, Jenny Edwards, Heather Grabbe, Ronan Harrington, Ivo Mensch and Jonathan Rowson for their contributions and advice.

Endless thanks also to the scholars, practitioners and champions of mindfulness who have lent their time and insight to this process. Thank you Ruth Baer, Trish Bartley, Stephen Batchelor, Vishvapani Blomfield, Roger Bretherton, Vidyamala Burch, Rebecca Crane, Chris Cullen, Luke Fortmann, Jim Gimian, Ed Halliwell, Jon Kabat-Zinn, Joel Levy, Michelle Levy, Rachel Lilley, Rhonda Magee, Ruth Ormston, Richard Reoch, John Roy, Otto Simonsson, Anne Speckens, Sander Tideman, Jutta Tobias, Caroline Voldstad, Jenny Wilks, Mark Williams and Tessa Watt.

About The Mindfulness Initiative

The Mindfulness Initiative is a policy institute dedicated to contemplative practice in politics and public life. It originated through a programme of mindfulness teaching for politicians in the UK Parliament, and provides the secretariat to the Mindfulness All-Party Parliamentary Group. Working with legislators around the world who practice mindfulness, we help to make capacities of heart and mind serious considerations of public policy. Visit www.themindfulnessinitiative.org to find out more.

About the Authors

Jamie Bristow is Director of the Mindfulness Initiative. Since 2013 he has worked in research and advocacy around the skilful adoption of mindfulness practice in society.

Rosie Bell is a writer and communications consultant, and copywriter for the Mindfulness Initiative. A philosophy graduate, performer and mindfulness teacher, she writes for global charities and wellbeing innovators.

Dan Nixon is a writer and researcher with ten years' experience in policy work at the Bank of England. He currently leads research projects for the Mindfulness Initiative and Perspectiva.

Please support our work

The Mindfulness Initiative doesn't receive any public funding and in order to retain its neutral and trusted advisory position in the sector cannot generate revenue from competitive products or services. As such, we are entirely dependent on charitable gifts for sustaining our work. If you found this discussion paper helpful, please consider making a contribution. Visit www.themindfulnessinitiative.org/appeal/donate to make a one-time or recurring donation.

Appendix 1 – Further reading & listening

The following texts, videos and podcasts have been influential on the thinking of the authors and we include them here for transparency and general interest. However, these references are unlikely to be properly representative of the diverse ideas and people working in the space, and we do not agree with or endorse everything contained within them. They should not be considered formal recommendations from the Mindfulness Initiative but merely personal suggestions for further enquiry. Please see electronic version available through our website for direct hyperlinks.

1. The mind and the world it creates
2. Meaning and the meta-crisis
3. Bildung / psychological development / moral, civic and systems education
4. Metamodern thought
5. Mindfulness and training ourselves for change

The mind and the world it creates

RSA Animate: The Divided Brain - Iain McGilchrist, RSA, 2011 [Video]
In this new RSA Animate, renowned psychiatrist and writer Iain McGilchrist explains how our 'divided brain' has profoundly altered human behaviour, culture and society.

Divided Brain, Divided World: Why The Best Part Of Us Struggles To Be Heard - Jonathan Rowson, Iain McGilchrist, RSA, 2013 [PDF]
"The discussion and reflections that follow feature an inquiry into a singularly profound, complex and fascinating thesis about the relationship between our brains and the world. Through this inquiry, I attempt to illustrate what a mature discussion about the social and political relevance of neuroscience might look like."

How To Do Nothing: Resisting the Attention Economy - Jenny Odell, 2019 [Book]
Nothing is harder to do these days than nothing. We find every last minute captured, optimised, or appropriated as a financial resource for the technologies we use daily. We consume algorithmic versions of ourselves, submit our free time to numerical evaluation, and maintain personal brands in digital space. After the American presidental election of 2016, Jenny Odell felt so overstimunated and disoriented by information, misinformation, and the expressions of others, that reality itself seemed to slip away. How To Do Nothing is her action plan for resistance. Drawing on the ethos of tech culture, a background in the arts, and personal storytelling, Jenny Odell makes a powerful argument for refusal: refusal to believe that our lives are instruments to be optimised.

The Patterning Instinct - Jeremy Lent, 2017 [Book]
In 1405, Admiral Zheng set off from China with the greatest armada in history, leading three hundred magnificent ships on a thirty year odyssey to distant lands as far afield as Africa. Later that century, Columbus landed in the New World with three barely seaworthy boats. Zheng's armada, for all its grandeur, left virtually no imprint on the world while Columbus changed the entire course of history. Why? The Patterning Instinct provides a new answer to this question with a simple but compelling theme: Culture shapes values, and those values shape history.

TAWAI - Bruce Parry, 2017 [Feature documentary]

Tawai is a word the nomadic hunter gatherers of Borneo use to describe the connection they feel to their forest home. In this dreamy, philosophical and sociological look at life, Bruce Parry (of the BBC's Tribe, Amazon & Arctic) embarks on an immersive odyssey to explore the different ways that humans relate to nature and how this influences the way we create our societies.

Corona: A Tale Of Two Systems. Part One - Bonnita Roy, Emerge, 2020 [Web article]

Huddled in our homes, we are experiencing two very different kinds of systems. One at risk of collapse, the other ancient, resilient and based on pro-social values and collective intelligence.

The World We Create: From God to Market - Tomas Björkman, 2019 [Book]

In The World We Create, Tomas Björkman takes readers on a journey through history, economics, sociology, developmental psychology and philosophy, to illuminate where we have come from and how we have reached this breaking point. He offers new perspectives on the world we have created and suggests how we can achieve a more meaningful, sustainable world in the future.

Inside-out sustainability: The neglect of inner worlds - Christopher D. Ives, Rebecca Freeth & Joern Fischer, 2020 [Open access academic paper]

In the context of continuing ecosystem degradation and deepening socio-economic inequality, sustainability scientists must question the adequacy of current scholarship and practice. We argue that pre-occupation with external phenomena and collective social structures has led to the neglect of people's 'inner worlds'—their emotions, thoughts, identities and beliefs. These lie at the heart of actions for sustainability, and have powerful transformative capacity for system change.

Meaning and the meta-crisis

The War on Sensemaking - Daniel Schmachtenberger, Rebel Wisdom, 2019 [Video]

What can we trust? Why is the 'information ecology' so damaged, and what would it take to make it healthy? This is a fundamental question, because without good sensemaking, we cannot even begin to act in the world. It is also a central concern in what many are calling the "meaning crisis", because what is meaningful is connected to what is real. Daniel Schmachtenberger is an evolutionary philosopher - his central interest is civilization design: developing new capacities for sense-making and choice-making, individually and collectively, to support conscious sustainable evolution.

We Can No Longer Save The World By Playing By The Rules - Tomas Bjorkman, Emerge, 2019 [Web article, talk transcript]

Especially in times of crisis, the systems we live in need to learn to organise in new, more complex and deeper ways, or they will break down.

The Politics Of Waking Up 1: Power And Possibility In The Fractal Age - Indra Adnan, Emerge, 2019 [Web article]

In this series for Emerge Indra Adnan, founder of the Alternative UK, will be exploring what is emerging in politics at this crucial moment in human history.

Why We Need Collective Intelligence During Global Collapse - Jordan Hall, 2017 [Podcast]

We are facing a potentially apocalyptic scenario for our world for three main reasons. We have become very powerful as a species, but we are not wise enough to handle that power. The second factor is our relationship to ourselves. Our governments, our peacemaking methods and our relationship to the rest of humanity are not well suited to the pace of change in our world today. Finally, we have an immature relationship to our technology, from mobile phones to nuclear weapons. All these three factors can create catastrophic and potentially existential outcomes for the whole humanity.

Ep. 1 - Awakening from the Meaning Crisis - Introduction - John Vervaeke, 2019 [Video]

Part 1 of John Vervaeke's lecture series on how cognitive science, existential philosophy, Buddhism, Hellenistic philosophy and psychedelics can be used to address the meaning crisis. John Vervaeke, PhD is an award-winning lecturer at the University of Toronto in the departments of psychology, cognitive science and Buddhist psychology. In this series Vervaeke will give the history of the meaning crisis, how it is affecting society today, and then give an account on how we can address this problem.

Bildung / psychological development / moral, civic and systems education

Bildung in the 21st Century: why sustainable prosperity depends upon reimagining education - Jonathan Rowson, CUSP, 2019 [PDF]

Bildung is a Germanic term with English and Greek roots and Nordic and American fruits. It describes a sense of fulfilling one's nature or purpose in response to the challenges of a particular historical and societal context. Bildung entails a dynamic world view that values independence of mind and spirit grounded in ecological and social interdependence. The premise of this essay is that we need to reconsider Bildung today because the challenge of 'understanding' in Understanding Sustainable Prosperity is pivotally important. The complexity of the world is overwhelming the complexity of our minds, and addressing that challenge is fundamental to our attempts to create a viable and desirable future.

Preparing for a Confusing Future Complexity, Warm Data and Education - Nora Bateson, Medium, 2018/2020 [Web article]

Putting the world back together now from the fragmented, decontextualized and silo-ed bits it has been broken into is a challenge that rests on the possibility of intergenerational collaborative exploration. To form and find interconnections will require humility and a new kind of attention to interdependent processes in complex systems. New sensitivity will be needed, new perception, new language, new ideas. If the human species is to continue, the way in which we consider ourselves in relation to each other, and the environment must evolve.

The Meta-Crisis is a Human Development Crisis: Education in a Time Between Worlds - Zachary Stein, Emerge Podcast, 2019 [Podcast]

Zak is a writer, educator and futurist working to bring a greater sense of sanity and justice to education. We chat about why the meta-crisis is fundamentally an educational crisis, a metamodern vision for the future of education, the difference between education and schooling, how to build an education system that can prepare humans for an unknowable and rapidly changing future, the postmodern erosion of 'teacherly authority', the relationship between education, passion, curiosity, and eros, and the possibility of education becoming a collective movement of soul-making.

A Larger Us - Alex Evans, The Collective Psychology Project, 2019 [PDF]

We're poised between two futures. One's the breakdown scenario. Climate chaos, extinction, scarcity, inequality, tribalism, collapse. This paper's about how we get to the other one: the breakthrough scenario. A future of safety, restoration, and flourishing, for us and for the world. Whether we make it there depends primarily on what goes on inside our minds. Whether we're able to manage our mental and emotional states, at a moment of extraordinary turbulence. Whether we reach for the right stories to explain what's happening at this moment in history. Whether enough of us see ourselves as part of a Larger Us instead of a them-and-us, or just an atomised "I". Our future depends, in other words, on collective psychology.

The Nordic Secret: A European story of beauty and freedom - Lene Rachel Andersen & Tomas Björkman, 2019 [Book]

How do societies go through major technological, economic and structural changes peacefully? The Nordic Secret explores how Denmark, Norway and Sweden went from poor feudal agricultural societies to rich industrialized democracies thanks to the German educational concept of Bildung. The book also investigates the close relationship between Bildung and contemporary developmental psychology, i.e. the concepts of "ego-development" and "transformative learning". The Nordic Secret concludes with a discussion about what we can learn from this positive transformation and how to apply it in the current global crises.

Education in a Time Between Worlds: Essays on the Future of Schools, Technology, and Society - Zachary Stein, 2019 [Book]

*Our world is currently undergoing major transformations, from climate change and politics to agriculture and economics. The world we have known is disappearing and a new world is being born. The subjects taught in schools and universities today are becoming irrelevant at faster and faster rates. Not only are we facing complex challenges of unprecedented size and scope, we're also facing a learning and capacity deficit that threatens the future of civilization. Also - **If education is not the answer you are asking the wrong question - ZS, 2019** [PDF]*

Metamodern thought

The beauty of a both/and mind: How can we find our way out of the impasse that stymies action on the really big issues of the day? - Michael Edwards, openDemocracy, 2018 [Web article]

...Any civil society or democracy worthy of the name needs both/and thinkers to animate its institutions. Otherwise separation will be permanent. That doesn't mean that everyone agrees on every issue, but it does require some agreement on how disagreement should be handled—as an invitation to deeper dialogue instead of a prelude to further fractures. This is exceptionally challenging because it runs counter to the realities of modern politics, media and knowledge production, but the other options are much, much worse: a slide into authoritarianism, enforced artificial unity, or permanent division. Faced by these 'beasts,' there's beauty in a both/and mind.

David Foster Wallace: The Problem with Irony - Will Schoder (2016) [Video]

What is Metamoderism? - Metamoderna [Web page]

Metamodern philosophy enters the scene only once the Internet and the social media have become truly dominant factors in people's lives and when many of us no longer partake directly in the production and distribution of industrial goods. It is a worldview which combines the modern faith in progress with the postmodern critique. What you get then, is a view of reality in which people are on a long, complex developmental journey towards greater complexity and existential depth.

The Listening Society & The Nordic Ideology: A Guide to Metamodern Politics Books 1 & 2 - Hanzi Freinacht [Book]

As we move from the industrial age and its nation state to an internet age with a globalized postindustrial market a question presents itself: What is the next major developmental stage of society after the liberal democracy with a balance between capitalism and welfare state? In this book Hanzi Freinacht offers a compelling answer to this question. We are reaching the limits of modern society and we must work to achieve a metamodern society, that is, a society which goes beyond modern life and its institutions. The metamodern society of the future is a listening society; a society more sensitive to the inner dimensions of human beings.

Metamodernity: Meaning and hope in a complex world - Lene Rachel Andersen (2019) [Book]
Technological development, climate change and globalization are challenging the national institutions and modes of governance we created during the industrial era. Our old knowledge and general understanding of the world do not provide sufficient answers anymore. In order to maintain meaningful lives, social calm and liberal democracy, we need to upgrade our meaning making to match the complexity of the world we are creating. Metamodernity is an alternative to both modernity and postmodernism, a cultural code that presents itself as an opportunity if we work deliberately towards it.

What is Metamodern? - whatismetamodern.com (artistic / aesthetic movement) [Website]
The central motivation of metamodernism is to protect interior, subjective felt experience from the ironic distance of postmodernism, the scientific reductionism of modernism, and the pre-personal inertia of tradition.

Introduction: Metamodernism - Dennis Kersten & Usha Wilbers (2018) [Academic article]
This special issue on Metamodernist literature in English comes at a moment when the academic debate about the concept is beginning to emerge and take shape. As these five essays demonstrate, the "Metamodernism" label—and its relationship to the supposed demise of Postmodernism and resurfacing of Modernism—sometimes yields clashing interpretations.

Mindfulness and training ourselves for change

Mindfulness In A Digital Era - Dr. Saki Santorelli, WGS, 2018 [Video]

Defining Sovereignty - Jordan Hall, 2018 [Video]
Sovereignty as a concept is crucial to help people improve their lives and adaptability. Jordan Greenhall helps to define the term along with the pillars that make up the concept. These pillars include accurately perceiving the world, making sense of those perceptions, making good choices based off of those perceptions, and finally acting on them.

Mindfulness for All: The Wisdom to Transform the World - Jon Kabat-Zinn, 2019 [Book]
In the fourth of these books, Mindfulness for All (which was originally published as Part VII and Part VIII of Coming to Our Senses), Kabat-Zinn focuses on how mindfulness really can be a tool to transform the world-- explaining how democracy thrives in a mindful context, and why mindfulness is a vital tool for both personal and global understanding and action in these tumultuous times.

Foreword: Seeds of a necessary global renaissance in the making: the refining of psychology's understanding of the nature of mind, self, and embodiment through the lens of mindfulness and its origins at a key inflection point for the species - Jon Kabat-Zinn, 2019 [Academic article]
Foreword to the special edition of the 2019 Current Opinion in Psychology special edition on Mindfulness.

The road beyond McMindfulness: What can we learn from 22 articles on mindfulness and social change? Michael Edwards, openDemocracy, 2020 [Web article]
Over the past few years there's been increasing interest in exploring one particular kind of practice called 'mindfulness' - "the basic human ability to be fully present, aware of where we are and what we're doing, and not overly reactive or overwhelmed by what's going on around us." It seems clear that strengthening these capacities is a useful thing to do for individuals, but can mindfulness also play a role in promoting broader social change? What can the articles we've published tell us about the answers to that question?

Contemplative Sustainable Futures [Website]

Humanity is facing increasingly complex environmental and sustainability challenges. Current coordination mechanisms, problem-solving strategies, and modes of scientific inquiry, teaching and learning appear insufficient to address these challenges. As a result, individual inner dimensions and transformation (embodied in notions such as consciousness, mindfulness and compassion) are emerging as a potential new area of exploration. The Contemplative Sustainable Futures Program was set up to explore this new area and create space and opportunities for learning, networking and knowledge development on these issues.

Mindfully Facing Climate Change - Bhikkhu Analayo, 2019 [Book]

In Mindfully Facing Climate Change, Bhikkhu Analayo offers a response to the challenges of climate change that is grounded in the teachings of early Buddhism and mindfulness meditation. Based on employing the teaching of the four noble truths as its main framework, it places facing climate change within the context of the eightfold path and provides detailed meditation instructions on how to build up mental resilience and balance.

Active Hope: How To Face The Mess We're In Without Going Crazy - Joanna Macy and Chris Johnstone, 2011 [Book]

Active Hope is about finding, and offering, our best response to the crisis of sustainability unfolding in our world. It offers tools that help us face the mess we're in, as well as find and play our role in the collective transition, or Great Turning, to a life-sustaining society.

Mindful of Race: Understanding and Transforming Habits of Harm: Transforming Racism from the Inside Out - Ruth King, 2018 [Book]

"Racism is a heart disease," writes Ruth King, "and it's curable." Exploring a crucial topic seldom addressed in meditation instruction, this revered teacher takes to her pen--to shine a compassionate, provocative, and practical light into a deeply neglected and world-changing domain profoundly relevant to all of us. In her newest publication, Mindful of Race, Ruth King invites us to: Tend first to our suffering and confusion, listen to what it is trying to teach us, and direct its energies most effectively for change.

The Inner Work of Racial Justice: Healing Ourselves and Transforming Our Communities Through Mindfulness - Rhonda Magee, 2019. [Book]

When conflict and division are everyday realities, our instincts tell us to close ranks, to find the safety of our own tribe, and to blame others. This book profoundly shows that in order to have the difficult conversations required for working toward racial justice, inner work is essential. Through the practice of embodied mindfulness--paying attention to our thoughts, feelings, and physical sensations in an open, nonjudgmental way--we increase our emotional resilience, recognize our own biases, and become less reactive when triggered.

The Mindfulness and Social Change Network [Website]

We are a global community exploring the potential for secular mindfulness training and practice to contribute to more sustainable, caring and socially just societies. We believe the human capacity for mindful awareness is vital for effective responses to social, economic and environmental challenges; and that mindfulness practice, courses and communities need to be responsive to the social and political context of individual stress, wellbeing and change.

Social Mindfulness: A Guide to meditation from Mindfulness-Based Organisational Education - Mark Leonard, 2019 [Book]

'Social Mindfulness' explains how we create a sense of self in relationship to others. Mindfulness practice enables us to diffuse the sense of a separate self and work with others in the service of collective interests. The book acts as a support to Mindfulness-Based Organisational Education (MBOE) as well as explaining the theory that underpins 'social mindfulness'.

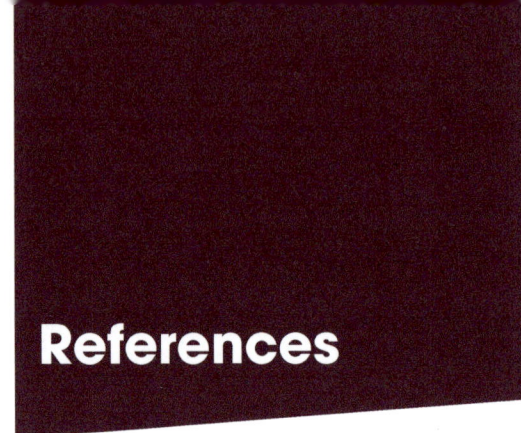

References

1   Ord, T. (2020). Existential risk and the future of Humanity. Bloomsbury, London, UK.

2   Stockholm Resilience Centre, Stockholm University. The nine planetary boundaries. Found at https://www.stockholmresilience.org/research/planetary-boundaries/planetary-boundaries/about-the-research/the-nine-planetary-boundaries.html

3   Wallace-Wells, D. (2019). The Uninhabitable Earth: A Story of the Future. Penguin, Random House. UK

4   Andersen, LR., (2017) Björkman, T. The Nordic Secret. A European story of beauty and freedom.

5   Johnstone, C. (2018). A Necessary "Growing Up" as a Species: An introduction to the concept of Cultural Maturity Part Three.

6   Freinacht, H. (2017). The Listening Society. A Metamodern Guide to Politics Book One. (1st ed.). Metamoderna.

7   Tegmark, M., Et al. (2017). Autonomous Weapons: An Open Letter From Ai & Robotics Researchers. Future of Life Institute. Retrieved from https://futureoflife.org/open-letter-autonomous-weapons/

    Bridge, M. (2017). Killer robots 'will cause war on a vast scale'. The Times, London. Retrieved from: https://www.thetimes.co.uk/article/elon-musk-among-technology-experts-calling-for-ban-on-killer-robo

8   Harari, Y.N. (2018). 21 Lessons for the 21st Century. Penguin Random House, London. p87.

9   Schlosser, M., (2019). Agency. Stanford Encyclopedia of Philosophy. Retrieved from: https://plato.stanford.edu/entries/agency/

10 Schmachtenberger, D., (2017). Advancing Human Sovereignty. Retrieved from: https://civilizationemerging.com/advancing-human-sovereignty/

11 Purser, R. (2019). The Mindfulness Conspiracy. The Guardian, retrieved from: www.theguardian.com/lifeandstyle/2019/jun/14/the-mindfulness-conspiracy-capitalist-spirituality

12 Reinaa, C.S., Kudesiab, R.S.,(2020). Wherever you go, there you become: How mindfulness arises in everyday situations. Organizational Behavior and Human Decision Processes. 159, p78-96.

13 Sangvi, M., Bristow, J., Bell, R., (2019). Fieldbook for Mindfulness Innovators. The Mindfulness Initiative, Sheffield UK.

14 Kenrick, D., Griskevicius, V., Neuberg, S., & Schaller, M. (2010). Renovating the Pyramid of Needs. Perspectives on Psychological Science, 5(3), 292-314.

15 Hadot, P. (1995). Philosophy as a Way of Life. Blackwell. Oxford, UK.

16 James, W., (1890) The Principles of Psychology. Retrieved from Classics in the History of Psychology: https://psychclassics.yorku.ca/James/Principles/prin11.htm

17 Noah, S., & Mangun, G. (2020). Recent evidence that attention is necessary, but not sufficient, for conscious perception. Annals of the New York Academy of Sciences, 1464(1), 52-63.

18 | Dehaene, S. (2020). How We Learn: The New Science of Education and the Brain, Chapter 7: Attention. Penguin

19 | Dijksterhuis, A. & Aarts, H. (2010). Goals, Attention, and (Un)Consciousness. Annual Review of Psychology. 61:1, 467-490.

20 | Wu, T. (2016). The Attention Merchants: How Our Time and Attention Are Gathered and Sold. Atlantic Analysis Corp. Norfolk, VA, United States

21 | Mark, G., Gudith, D., & Klocke, U. (2008). The cost of interrupted work. Proceeding of the Twenty-Sixth Annual CHI Conference on Human Factors in Computing Systems - CHI 08. doi: 10.1145/1357054.1357072

22 | Williams, J. (2018). Stand out of our light: Freedom and resistance in the attention economy. Cambridge University Press. Cambridge, UK.

23 | Manson, K. (2020). US intelligence warns about foreign election interference. The Financial Times. Retrieved from: https://www.ft.com/content/3d906d4e-f2f2-4228-998e-f971de3f4af8

24 | Oliver, M., (2020). Infrastructure and the Post-Truth Era: is Trump Twitter's Fault?. Postdigit Sci Educ 2, 17–38. https://doi.org/10.1007/s42438-019-00073-8

25 | Williams, J.M.G., (2009) .Mindfulness, Depression and Modes of Mind. Cogn Ther Res 32, 721. https://doi.org/10.1007/s10608-008-9204-z

26 | Greenberg, J., Romero, V., Elkin-Frankston, S., Bezdek, M., Schumacher, E., & Lazar, S. (2018). Reduced interference in working memory following mindfulness training is associated with increases in hippocampal volume. Brain Imaging and Behavior, 13(2), 366-376.

27 | Cásedas, L., Pirruccio, V., Vadillo, M., & Lupiáñez, J. (2020). Does Mindfulness Meditation Training Enhance Executive Control? A Systematic Review and Meta-Analysis of Randomized Controlled Trials in Adults. Mindfulness, 11(2), 411-424.

28 | Reinaa, C.S., Kudesiab, R.S.,(2020). Wherever you go, there you become: How mindfulness arises in everyday situations. Organizational Behavior and Human Decision Processes. 159, p78-96.

29 | Wu, T. (2016). The Attention Merchants: How Our Time and Attention Are Gathered and Sold. Atlantic Analysis Corp. Norfolk, VA, United States

30 | Killingsworth, M.A., Gilbert, D.T., (2010). A Wandering Mind Is an Unhappy Mind. Science: 932.

31 | Metzinger, T. (2013) The myth of cognitive agency: subpersonal thinking as a cyclically recurring loss of mental autonomy. Frontiers in Psychology. 4: 931. DOI=10.3389/fpsyg.2013.00931

32 | Turkle, S. (2011). Alone together: Why we expect more from technology and less from ourselves: New York: Basic Books

33 | Misra, S., Cheng, L., Genevie, J., Et al. (2014). The iPhone Effect: The Quality of In-Person Social Interactions in the Presence of Mobile Devices. Research Article. https://doi.org/10.1177/0013916514539755

34 | McDaniel, B. T., & Coyne, S. M. (2016). "Technoference": The interference of technology in couple relationships and implications for women's personal and relational well-being. Psychology of Popular MediaCulture, 5, 85.

35 | Sbarra, D., Briskin, J., & Slatcher, R. (2019). Smartphones and Close Relationships: The Case for an Evolutionary Mismatch. Perspectives on Psychological Science, 14(4), 596-618.

36 | Putnam, RD, (2000). Bowling Alone: The Collapse and Revival of American Community

37 | Gerst-Emerson, K., Jayawardhana, J., (2015). Loneliness as a public health issue: the impact of loneliness on health care utilization among older adults. American journal of public health vol. 105,5 (2015): 1013-9.

38	Harris, T., (2020). Can Truth Survive Big Tech? Rebel Wisom via YouTube. Retrieved from: https://www.youtube.com/watch?v=wHQQFOv7QgQ
39	Phillips, B. (2019), The Shifting Border Between Perception and Cognition. Noûs, 53: 316-346. doi:10.1111/nous.12218
40	Lupyan, G. (2015). Cognitive Penetrability of Perception in the Age of Prediction: Predictive Systems are Penetrable Systems. Review of Philosophy and Psychology, 6(4), 547-569.
41	Crane, R.S., Brewer, J., Feldman, C., Kabat-Zinn, J., Santorelli, S., Williams, J.M.G., Kuyken, W., (2017). What defines mindfulness-based programs? The warp and the weft. DOI: https://doi.org/10.1017/S0033291716003317
42	Feldman, C., Kuyken, W. (2019). Mindfulness: Ancient Wisdom Meets Modern Psychology. New York, NY, USA. The Guildford Press.}
43	Kuyken, W., Et al., (2010) How does mindfulness-based cognitive therapy work? Behaviour Research and Therapy. 48:11. 1105-1112.
44	McCown, D., Riebel, D., Micozzi, M. (2010) Teaching Mindfulness.
45	Burch, V. (2016). Meditation and the management of pain. In West, M. (Ed.), The Psychology of Meditation: Research and Practice (p164). Oxford University Press. Edited by Michael A. West Publisher: Oxford University Press. DOI: 10.1093/med:psych/9780199688906.001.0001
46	Crane, R.S., Brewer, J., Feldman, C., Kabat-Zinn, J., Santorelli, S., Williams, J.M.G., Kuyken, W., (2017). What defines mindfulness-based programs? The warp and the weft. DOI: https://doi.org/10.1017/S0033291716003317
47	Treves, I., Tello, L., Davidson, R., & Goldberg, S. (2019). The relationship between mindfulness and objective measures of body awareness: A meta-analysis. Scientific Reports, 9(1), 1-12.
48	Werner, N., Schweitzer, N., Meindl, T., Duschek, S., Kambeitz, J., & Schandry, R. (2013). Interoceptive awareness moderates neural activity during decision-making. Biological Psychology, 94(3), 498-506.
49	Jones, S., Bodie, G., & Hughes, S. (2019). The Impact of Mindfulness on Empathy, Active Listening, and Perceived Provisions of Emotional Support. Communication Research, 46(6), 838-865.
50	Trent, N., Park, C., Bercovitz, K., & Chapman, I. (2015). Trait Socio-Cognitive Mindfulness is Related to Affective and Cognitive Empathy. Journal of Adult Development, 23(1), 62-67.
51	Nadler, R., Carswell, J., & Minda, J. (2020). Online Mindfulness Training Increases Well-Being, Trait Emotional Intelligence, and Workplace Competency Ratings: A Randomized Waitlist-Controlled Trial. Frontiers in Psychology, 11,
52	Mayer, J., Salovey, P., & Caruso, D. (2008). Emotional Intelligence. American Psychologist, 63(6), 503-517.
53	Luberto, C., Shinday, N., Song, R., Philpotts, L., Park, E., Fricchione, G., & Yeh, G. (2017). A Systematic Review and Meta-analysis of the Effects of Meditation on Empathy, Compassion, and Prosocial Behaviors. Mindfulness, 9(3), 708-724.
54	Cheang, R., Gillions, A., & Sparkes, E. (2019). Do Mindfulness-Based Interventions Increase Empathy and Compassion in Children and Adolescents: A Systematic Review. Journal of Child and Family Studies, 28(7), 1765-1779.
55	Teper,R.; Inzlicht, M. (2013). Meditation, mindfulness and executive control: the importance of emotional acceptance and brain-based performance monitoring. Social Cognitive and Affective Neuroscience, 8:1, 85–92, https://doi.org/10.1093/scan/nss045
56	Karremans, J., Schellekens, M., & Kappen, G. (2017). Bridging the Sciences of Mindfulness and Romantic Relationships. Personality and Social Psychology Review, 21(1), 29-49. Khaddouma, A., Coop Gordon, K., & Strand, E. (2017). Mindful Mates: A Pilot Study of the Relational Effects of Mindfulness-Based Stress Reduction on Participants and Their Partners. Family Process, 56(3), 636-651.

57   Adam A. Kaya, A.A., Skarlicki, D.P., (2017). Cultivating a conflict-positive workplace: How mindfulness facilitates constructive conflict management. Organizational Behavior and Human Decision Processes journal homepage: www.elsevier.com/locate/obhdp

58   Kabat-Zinn, J. (1991). Full Catastrophe Living: Using the Wisdom of Your Body and Mind to Face Stress, Pain, and Illness. 33-40. Delta Trade Paperbacks, USA.

59   Kabat-Zinn, J., (1990). Full Catastrophe Living. Hachette.

60   Lueke, A., & Gibson, B. (2016). Brief Mindfulness Meditation Reduces Discrimination. Psychology of Consciousness: Theory, Research, and Practice, 3(1), 34-44.

61   Hopthrow, T., Hooper, N., Mahmood, L., Meier, B., & Weger, U. (2017). Mindfulness Reduces the Correspondence Bias. Quarterly Journal of Experimental Psychology, 70(3), 351-360.

62   Hafenbrack, A., Kinias, Z., & Barsade, S. (2014). Debiasing the Mind Through Meditation. Psychological Science, 25(2), 369-376.

63   Lueke, A., & Gibson, B. (2015). Mindfulness Meditation Reduces Implicit Age and Race Bias. Social Psychological and Personality Science, 6(3), 284-291.

64   Whitehead, M., et al. (2017). Neuroliberalism, New York: Routledge. Google Scholar.

65   Lilley, R (2020) Rethinking Government Capacities to Tackle Wicked Problems: Mind, Emotion, Bias and Decision-Making. An Experimental Trial using Mindfulness and Behavioural Economics. PhD thesis, Aberystwyth University.

66   Lueke, A., Gibson, B. (2014). Mindfulness Meditation Reduces Implicit Age and Race Bias: The Role of Reduced Automaticity of Responding, Soc. Psychol. And Personality Sci. 1, 5

67   Magee, R. (2016) The Way of ColorInsight: Understanding Race and Law Effectively through Mindfulness-Based ColorInsight Practices. 8 Geo. J. L. & Mod. Critical Race Persp. 251

68   Ostafin, B. D. (2015) and Lebuda, I., Zabelina, D. L., & Karwowski, M. (2016). Mind full of ideas: A meta-analysis of the mindfulness–creativity link. Personality and Individual Differences, 93, 22-26.

69   Berkovich-Ohana1, A., Glicksohn, J., Ben-Soussan, TD., Goldstein, A., (2016). Creativity Is Enhanced by Long-Term Mindfulness Training and Is Negatively Correlated with Trait Default-Mode-Related Low-Gamma Inter-Hemispheric Connectivity. Mindfulness. DOI 10.1007/s12671-016-0649-y

     Colzato, L., Szapora, A., Lippelt, D., & Hommel, B. (2014). Prior Meditation Practice Modulates Performance and Strategy Use in Convergent- and Divergent-Thinking Problems. Mindfulness, 8(1), 10-16.

70   Scharmer, O., (2016). Theory U: Leading from the Future as It Emerges.
Berrett-Koehler Publishers.

71   Cooper, J. (2007) Cognitive Dissonance: 50 Years of a Classic Theory. Sage Publications Ltd.

72   Olympic gold medallist Etienne Stott (2014). Retreived from huffingtonpost.co.uk/vogue-uk/vogue-arianna-huffington-headspace_b_5418740.html

73   Fraher, AL., Branicki, LJ., Grint, K. (2017). Mindfulness in Action: Discovering How U.S. Navy Seals Build Capacity for Mindfulness in High-Reliability Organizations (HROs). AMD, 3, 239–261, https://doi.org/10.5465/amd.2014.0146

74   Friesen, J., Laurin, K., Shepherd, S., Gaucher, D., & Kay, A. (2019). System justification: Experimental evidence, its contextual nature, and implications for social change. British Journal of Social Psychology, 58(2), 315-339.

75   Toffler, A. (1970) Future Shock. Random House.

76 | Simmel, G., (1903). The Metropolis and Mental Life. Blackwell Publishing. Retrieved from: https://www.blackwellpublishing.com/content/bpl_images/content_store/sample_chapter/0631225137/bridge.pdf

77 | Williams, J. (2018). Stand out of our light: Freedom and resistance in the attention economy. Cambridge University Press. Cambridge, UK.

78 | Baddeley, A. (1992). Working Memory: The Interface between Memory and Cognition. Journal of Cognitive Neuroscience, 4(3), 281-288.

79 | Jha, A., Witkin, J., Morrison, A., Rostrup, N., & Stanley, E. (2017). Short-Form Mindfulness Training Protects Against Working Memory Degradation over High-Demand Intervals. Journal of Cognitive Enhancement, 1(2), 154-171.

80 | Sandi, C. (2013). Stress and cognition. Wiley Interdisciplinary Reviews: Cognitive Science, 4(3), 245-261.

81 | Thoits, P. (2010). Stress and Health: Major Findings and Policy Implications. Journal of Health and Social Behavior, 51(1_suppl), S41-S53.

82 | Prinet, J., & Sarter, N. (2015). The Effects of High Stress on Attention. Proceedings of the Human Factors and Ergonomics Society Annual Meeting, 59(1), 1530-1534.

83 | Goldberg, SB., Tucker, RP.,Greene, PA., Davidson, RJ., Wampold, BE., Kearney, DJ., Simpson, TL. (2018) Mindfulness-based interventions for psychiatric disorders: A systematic review and meta-analysis. Clin Psychol Rev. 2018 Feb; 59: 52–60.

84 | Khoury, B., Sharmac, M., Rush, SE., Fourniere, C., (2015). Mindfulness-based stress reduction for healthy individuals: A meta-analysis. Journal of Psychosomatic Research. 78.6:519-528

Jayawardene, W., Lohrmann, D., Erbe, R., & Torabi, M. (2016). Effects of preventive online mindfulness interventions on stress and mindfulness: A meta-analysis of randomized controlled trials. Preventive Medicine Reports, 5, 150-159.

85 | Pascoe, M.C, Thompson, D.R., Jenkins, Z.M., Ski, C.F., Mindfulness mediates the physiological markers of stress: Systematic review and meta-analysis. J Psychiatr Res; 95:156-178. doi: 10.1016/j.jpsychires.2017.08.004.

86 | Jha, A., Morrison, A., Parker, S., & Stanley, E. (2016). Practice Is Protective: Mindfulness Training Promotes Cognitive Resilience in High-Stress Cohorts. Mindfulness, 8(1), 46-58.

Jha, A., Zanesco, A., Denkova, E., Morrison, A., Ramos, N., Chichester, K., Gaddy, J., & Rogers, S. (2020). Bolstering Cognitive Resilience via Train-the-Trainer Delivery of Mindfulness Training in Applied High-Demand Settings. Mindfulness, 11(3), 683-697.

87 | Cásedas, L., Pirruccio, V., Vadillo, M., & Lupiáñez, J. (2020). Does Mindfulness Meditation Training Enhance Executive Control? A Systematic Review and Meta-Analysis of Randomized Controlled Trials in Adults. Mindfulness, 11(2), 411-424.

88 | Jha, A., Morrison, A., Parker, S., & Stanley, E. (2016). Practice Is Protective: Mindfulness Training Promotes Cognitive Resilience in High-Stress Cohorts. Mindfulness, 8(1), 46-58.

89 | Purser, R. (2019). The mindfulness conspiracy. The Guardian. Retrieved from: www.theguardian.com/lifeandstyle/2019/jun/14/the-mindfulness-conspiracy-capitalist-spirituality

90 | Chen, C., & Gorski, P. (2015). Burnout in Social Justice and Human Rights Activists: Symptoms, Causes and Implications. Journal of Human Rights Practice, 7(3), 366-390.

91 | Gorski, P. (2015). Relieving Burnout and the "Martyr Syndrome" Among Social Justice Education Activists: The Implications and Effects of Mindfulness. The Urban Review, 47(4), 696-716.

Driscoll, D. (2020). When Ignoring the News and Going Hiking Can Help You Save the World: Environmental Activist Strategies for Persistence. Sociological Forum, 35(1), 189-206.

92 | Schudson, M., (2019). The Fall, Rise, and Fall of Media Trust. Columbia Journal Review. Retrieved from: https://www.cjr.org/special_report/the-fall-rise-and-fall-of-media-trust.php

93 | Williams, E., (2020). The UK: A parable of mistrust. Edelman. Retrieved from: https://www.edelman.com/research/uk-parable-distrust

94 | Phillips, W., (2020). You May Not Even Know You're Spreading Lies. Wired. Retrieved from: https://www.wired.com/story/you-may-not-even-know-youre-spreading-lies/

95 | What is Information Ecology. IGI Global. Retrieved from: https://www.igi-global.com/dictionary/developing-creativity-and-learning-design-by-information-and-communication-technology-ict-in-developing-contexts/60255

96 | Schmachtenberger, D., (2019). The War on Sensemaking. Rebel Wisdom via YouTube. Retrieved from: https://www.youtube.com/watch?v=7LqaotiGWjQ

97 | Bjorkman, T. (2018). How to use personal, inner development to build strong democracies | Tomas Björkman | TEDxBerlin. Retrieved from: https://www.youtube.com/watch?time_continue=92&v=b4dFsHgd1rQ&feature=emb_logo

98 | Stein, Z., (2019). If education is not the answer you are asking the wrong question: why it's time to see planetary crises as a species-wide learning opportunity. Perspectiva. Retrieved from: http://www.zakstein.org/wp-content/uploads/2014/10/If-education-is-not-the-answer-you-are-asking-the-wrong-question.pdf

99 | Kabat-Zinn, J., (1990, 2013). Full Catastrophe Living. Piaktus. Position 9103/12046 in eBook version.

100 | Bateson, N., (2020). Preparing for a Confusing Future Complexity, Warm Data and Education. Medium. Retrieved from: https://medium.com/@norabateson/preparing-for-a-confusing-future-complexity-warm-data-and-education-8eaae6b09eef

101 | Helbling, T., (2020). Externalities: Prices Do Not Capture All Costs. International Monetary Fund. Retrieved from: https://www.imf.org/external/pubs/ft/fandd/basics/external.htm

102 | Tickell, P., (2020). I need you to read this and decide about Coronavirus: Approaching the pandemic with a systems-thinking lens. Retrieved from: https://medium.com/@phoebetickell/i-need-you-to-read-this-and-decide-about-coronavirus-6dd184745b33

103 | Newen, De Bruin and Gallagher. (2018). The Oxford Handbook of 4E Cognition, Oxford Library of Psychology. Oxford University Press.

104 | Ref Teasdale & Chaskalson 2013 in Williams & Kabat-Zinn ed. 2013. Also potentially Teasdale and Barnard's papers on Interacting Cognitive Subsystems [ICS] e.g. https://www.tandfonline.com/doi/abs/10.1080/02699939108411021

105 | Yama, H., Zakaria, N. (2019). Explanations for cultural differences in thinking: Easterners' dialectical thinking and Westerners' linear thinking Journal of Cognitive Psychology. 31(4); 487-506. https://doi.org/10.1080/20445911.2019.1626862.

106 | McGilchrist, I. (2012). The Master and His Emissary. Yale University Press; 2nd edition.

107 | Panksepp, J., (2010) Affective neuroscience of the emotional BrainMind: evolutionary perspectives and implications for understanding depression. Dialogues Clin Neurosci. 2010 Dec; 12(4): 533–545.

108 | Langer, E., & Moldoveanu, M. (2000). The Construct of Mindfulness. Journal of Social Issues, 56(1).

Block-Lerner, J., Adair, C., Plumb, J., Rhatigan, D., & Orsillo, S. (2007). The case for mindfulness-based approaches in the cultivation of empathy: Does nonjudgmental, present-moment awareness increase capacity for perspective-taking and empathic concern?. Journal of Marital and Family Therapy, 33(4).

Karremans, J., van Schie, H., van Dongen, I., Kappen, G., Mori, G., van As, S., ten Bokkel, I., & van der Wal, R. (2019). Is Mindfulness Associated With Interpersonal Forgiveness?. Emotion, 1

109 | Hölzel, B., Lazar, S., Gard, T., Schuman-Olivier, Z., Vago, D., & Ott, U. (2011). How Does Mindfulness Meditation Work? Proposing Mechanisms of Action From a Conceptual and Neural Perspective. Perspectives on Psychological Science, 6(6), 537-559.

110   Rowson, J., (2015). Spiritualise. RSA. London, UK

111   Shapiro, L. (2019). Embodied Cognition: 2nd Ed. Routledge. New York, NY, USA.

112   Vervaeke, J. (2020) The Master, his Emissary & the Meaning Crisis, Iain McGilchrist & John Vervaeke. YouTube. Retrieved from: https://youtu.be/JdB-BMdgFbk

113   Bihari, J., & Mullan, E. (2012). Relating Mindfully: A Qualitative Exploration of Changes in Relationships Through Mindfulness-Based Cognitive Therapy. Mindfulness, 5(1), 46-59.

114   Allen, M., Bromley, A., Kuyken, W., and Sonnenberg, S.J., (2009). Participants' Experiences of Mindfulness-Based Cognitive Therapy: "It Changed Me in Just about Every Way Possible". Behavioural and Cognitive Psychotherapy, 2009, 37, 413–430 doi:10.1017/S135246580999004X

115   Dunoon, D., Langer, E., (2011). "Mindfulness and Leadership: Opening up to Possibilities." Integral Leadership Review 11 (5) (October):1-15.

116   Carson, S.H., Langer, E.J. Mindfulness and self-acceptance. J Rat-Emo Cognitive-Behav Ther 24, 29–43 (2006). https://doi.org/10.1007/s10942-006-0022-5

117   Moore, A., Peter Malinowski, P., (2009) Meditation, mindfulness and cognitive flexibility. Consciousness and Cognition 18 (2009) 176–186. doi:10.1016/j.concog.2008.12.008

118   Scott, W.A., (1962). Cognitive complexity and cognitive flexibility. Sociometry. 25 (4): 405–414. doi:10.2307/2785779. JSTOR 2785779.

119   Meirana, N., Diamond, G.M., Toder, D., Nemets, B., (2011). Cognitive rigidity in unipolar depression and obsessive compulsive disorder: Examination of task switching, Stroop, working memory updating and post-conflict adaptation. Psychiatry Research. 185, 1–2, 149-156.

        Arlt, J., Yiu, A., Eneva, K., Dryman, M.T., Heimberg, R.G., Chen, E.Y., (2016). Contributions of cognitive inflexibility to eating disorder and social anxiety symptoms. Eating Behaviors. 21: 30-32. https://doi.org/10.1016/j.eatbeh.2015.12.008

120   Crane, R.S., (2017) Implementing Mindfulness in the Mainstream: Making the Path by Walking It. Mindfulness 8, 585–594. https://doi.org/10.1007/s12671-016-0632-7

121   Shonin, E., & Gordon, W. (2016). The Mechanisms of Mindfulness in the Treatment of Mental Illness and Addiction. International Journal of Mental Health and Addiction, 14(5), 844-849.

122   Bristow, J. (2019). Mindfulness in politics and public policy. Current Opinion in Psychology, 28:87–91 https://doi.org/10.1016/j.copsyc.2018.11.003

123   Schwartz, S. H. (2012). An Overview of the Schwartz Theory of Basic Values. Online Readings in Psychology and Culture, 2(1). https://doi.org/10.9707/2307-0919.1116

124   Holmes, T., Blackmore, E., Hawkins, R., Wakeford, T., (2011). The Common Cause Handbook. Public Interest Research Centre. Machynlleth, Wales.

125   R. S., Kuyken, W., Hastings, R. P., Rothwell, N., & Williams, J. M. G. (2010). Training teachers to deliver mindfulness-based interventions: Learning from the UK experience. Mindfulness, 1(2), 74-86.]

126   Hayes, S., Pistorello, J., & Levin, M. (2012). Acceptance and Commitment Therapy as a Unified Model of Behavior Change. The Counseling Psychologist, 40(7), 976-1002.

127   Manlick, C., Cochran, S., & Koon, J. (2012). Acceptance and Commitment Therapy for Eating Disorders: Rationale and Literature Review. Journal of Contemporary Psychotherapy, 43(2), 115-122.

128   Vowles, K.E., Wetherell, J.L., Sorrell, J.T., (2009) Targeting Acceptance, Mindfulness, and Values-Based Action in Chronic Pain: Findings of Two Preliminary Trials of an Outpatient Group-Based Intervention. Cognitive and Behavioral Practice 16 (2009) 49–58

129   A-tjak, J. G., Davis, M. L., Morina, N., Powers, M. B., Smits, J. A., & Emmelkamp, P. M. (2015). A meta-analysis of the efficacy of acceptance and commitment therapy for clinically relevant mental and physical health problems. Psychotherapy and Psychosomatics, 84(1), 30-36.

130   Baer, R. (2015). Ethics, Values, Virtues, and Character Strengths in Mindfulness-Based Interventions: a Psychological Science Perspective. Mindfulness, 6(4), 956-969.

131   Ivtzan, I., Niemiec, R. M., & Briscoe, C. (2016). A study investigating the effects of Mindfulness-Based Strengths Practice (MBSP) on wellbeing. International Journal of Wellbeing, 6(2), 1-13. doi:10.5502/ijw.v6i2.557

132   Leonard, M., (2019). Social Mindfulness: A guide to meditations from Mindfulness-Based Organisational Education. Mindfulness Connected Limited. Oxford, UK.

       Barker, MJ., (2015). Social Mindfulness. Retrieved from: https://rewriting-the-rules.com/wp-content/uploads/2015/07/socialmindfulnesszine.pdf

133   Brewer, J., (2017). Loneliness: The Cultural Pandemic. The Big Smoke, America. Retrieved from: https://thebigsmoke.com/2017/03/30/loneliness-cultural-pandemic/

134   Dunbar, RIM. (2003).The social brain: mind, language, and society in evolutionary perspective. Annual review of anthropology.

135   Mller, Earl & Buschman, Timothy. (2015). Working Memory Capacity: Limits on the Bandwidth of Cognition. Daedalus. 144. 112-122. 10.1162/DAED_a_00320.

136   Woolley, A., Aggarwal, I., & Malone, T. (2015). Collective Intelligence and Group Performance. Current Directions in Psychological Science, 24(6), 420-424.

       Hall, J. (2017). 47: Jordan Greenhall - Why We Need Collective Intelligence During Global Collapse. 08'30". Future Thinkers podcast. Retrieved from: https://www.youtube.com/watch?v=mGNrf_nwKy4

137   Palese, A., (2018). The Irish abortion referendum: How a Citizens' Assembly helped to break years of political deadlock. The Electoral Reform Society. Retrieved via: https://www.electoral-reform.org.uk/the-irish-abortion-referendum-how-a-citizens-assembly-helped-to-break-years-of-political-deadlock/

138   The Citizens' Convention on Climate, what is it? Convention Citoyenne Pour Le Climat. Retrieved via: https://www.conventioncitoyennepourleclimat.fr/en/

139   Thai H., Im H., Kim Y. (2019) Pathways to Electronic Citizen Participation: Policy and Technological Arrangements in Korea. In: Farazmand A. (eds) Global Encyclopedia of Public Administration, Public Policy, and Governance. Springer, Cham. https://doi.org/10.1007/978-3-319-31816-5_3799-1

140   Miller, C. (2019). Taiwan is making democracy work again. It's time we paid attention. Wired Magazine. Retrieved from: https://www.wired.co.uk/article/taiwan-democracy-social-media

141   Leonard, A., (2020). How Taiwan's Unlikely Digital Minister Hacked the Pandemic. Wired Magazine. Retrieved from: https://www.wired.com/story/how-taiwans-unlikely-digital-minister-hacked-the-pandemic/

142   Weick, K. E., Sutcliffe, K. M., & Obstfeld, D., (1999). Organizing for High Reliability: Processes of Collective Mindfulness. In B. M. Staw & L. L. Cummings (Eds.), Research in Organizational Behavior (Vol. 21, pp. 81-123). Greenwich, CT: JAI Press, Inc.

143   Martini, J-P., Stephan, L., Tamdjidi, C., (2020) Tap Your Company's Collective Intelligence with Mindfulness. BCG.com. Retreived from: https://www.bcg.com/en-gb/publications/2020/tap-your-company-collective-intelligence-with-mindfulness.aspx

144   Schwartz, S., & Bilsky, W. (1987). Toward A Universal Psychological Structure of Human Values. Journal of Personality and Social Psychology, 53(3), 550-562.

145   Tan, C-M, (2014). Search Inside Yourself: The Unexpected Path to Achieving Success, Happiness (and World Peace). HarperOne; Reprint Edition.

146   Carter, A. & Tobias Mortlock, J. (2019). Mindfulness in the military: improving mental fitness in the UK Armed Forces using next generation team mindfulness training". Institute of Employment Studies project report 00090-5367

147   Skopeliti, C., (2019). Former Commons Speaker will issue plea for that 'personal courtesy should become guiding light in 2020'. The Guardian. Retrieved from: https://www.theguardian.com/politics/2019/dec/23/john-bercow-to-deliver-channel-4s-alternative-christmas-message; Russell, J. (2019). Brexit bearpit leaves no room for decent MPs. The Times. Retrieved from: https://www.thetimes.co.uk/edition/news/hatred-is-too-much-to-bear-for-principled-mps-l5zvms559

148   Bristow, J. (2019). Mindfulness in politics and public policy. Current Opinion in Psychology, 28:87–91 https://doi.org/10.1016/j.copsyc.2018.11.003

149   Horlacher, R. (2004) Bildung – A construction of a history of philosophy of education. Stud Philos Educ 23, 409–426. https://doi.org/10.1007/s11217-004-4452-1

150   Andersen, LR., (2017) Björkman, T. The Nordic Secret. A European story of beauty and freedom.

151   Rowson, J., (2019). Bildung in the 21st Century: why sustainable prosperity depends upon reimagining education. Centre for the Understanding of Sustainable Prosperity. Retrieved from: https://www.cusp.ac.uk/themes/m/essay-m1-9/

152   Freinacht, H., (c.2016). What is Metamodernism? Retrieved from: https://metamoderna.org/metamodernism/

153   Andersen, LR., (2019). Metamodernity: Meaning and hope in a complex world. Nordic Bildung

154   Edwards, M., (2018). The beauty of a both/and mind: How can we find our way out of the impasse that stymies action on the really big issues of the day? Retrieved from: https://www.opendemocracy.net/en/transformation/beauty-of-bothand-mind/

155   Freinacht, H. (2019). The Nordic Ideology: A Metamodern Guide to Politics, Book Two. Metamoderna.

156   Freinacht, H., (c.2016). What is Metamodernism? Retrieved from: https://metamoderna.org/metamodernism/

157   Segal, Z.V., Williams, M., Teasdale, J. (2013). Mindfulness-Based Cognitive Therapy. Chapter 16, page 338. The Guildford Press.

158   Hassan, L., Shiu, E., & Shaw, D. (2014). Who Says There is an Intention–Behaviour Gap? Assessing the Empirical Evidence of an Intention–Behaviour Gap in Ethical Consumption. Journal of Business Ethics, 136(2), 219-236.

159   Legge, M., (2019). Are We Done Fighting? Building Understanding in a World of Hate and Division. New Society Publishers.

160   Ludwig, V., Brown, K., & Brewer, J. (2020). Self-Regulation Without Force: Can Awareness Leverage Reward to Drive Behavior Change?. Perspectives on Psychological Science, 1

161   Jury, T., & Jose, P. (2018). Does Rumination Function as a Longitudinal Mediator Between Mindfulness and Depression?. Mindfulness, 10(6), 1091-1104.

162   Stanszus, L.S., Frank, P., Geiger, S.M., (2019). Healthy eating and sustainable nutrition through mindfulness? Mixed method results of a controlled intervention study. Appetite. 141: 104325. https://doi.org/10.1016/j.appet.2019.104325

      Warren, J., Smith, N., & Ashwell, M. (2017). A structured literature review on the role of mindfulness, mindful eating and intuitive eating in changing eating behaviours: Effectiveness and associated potential mechanisms. Nutrition Research Reviews, 30(2), 272-283. doi:10.1017/S0954422417000154

163   Ostafin, B., Bauer, C., & Myxter, P. (2012). Mindfulness Decouples the Relation Between Automatic Alcohol Motivation and Heavy Drinking. Journal of Social and Clinical Psychology, 31(7), 729-745.

164   Chatzisarantis, N., & Hagger, M. (2007). Mindfulness and the Intention-Behavior Relationship Within the Theory of Planned Behavior. Personality and Social Psychology Bulletin, 33(5), 663-676.

165   Bihari, J., & Mullan, E. (2012). Relating Mindfully: A Qualitative Exploration of Changes in Relationships Through Mindfulness-Based Cognitive Therapy. Mindfulness, 5(1), 46-59.

166 | Nock MK, Wedig MM, Holmberg EB, Hooley JM. (2010). The Emotion Reactivity Scale: Development, evaluation, and relation to self-injurious thoughts and behaviors. Behav Therapy. 39:107–16.

167 | Raes, F., Dewulf, D., Van Heeringen, C., & Williams, J. M. G. (2009). Mindfulness and reduced cognitive reactivity to sad mood: evidence from a correlational study and a nonrandomized waiting list controlled study. Behaviour Research and Therapy, 47(7), 623–7. http://doi.org/10.1016/j.brat.2009.03.007

168 | Gu, J., Strauss, C., Bond, R., Cavanagh, K. (2015). How do mindfulness-based cognitive therapy and mindfulness-based stress reduction improve mental health and wellbeing? A systematic review and meta-analysis of mediation studies. Clinical Psychology Review. 37, 1-12. https://www.sheffield.ac.uk/polopoly_fs/1.588515!/file/Guetal2015.pdf

169 | Feldman, G., Lavallee, J., Gildawie, K., & Greeson, J. (2016). Dispositional Mindfulness Uncouples Physiological and Emotional Reactivity to a Laboratory Stressor and Emotional Reactivity to Executive Functioning Lapses in Daily Life. Mindfulness, 7(2), 527-541.

170 | Peters, J. R., Erisman, S. M., Upton, B. T., Baer, R. A., & Roemer, L. (2011). A preliminary investigation of the relationships between dispositional mindfulness and impulsivity. Mindfulness, 2(4), 228-235.

171 | Scott-Hamilton, J., Schutte, N., & Brown, R. (2016). Effects of a Mindfulness Intervention on Sports-Anxiety, Pessimism, and Flow in Competitive Cyclists. Applied Psychology: Health and Well-Being, 8(1), 85-103.

Jackson, S. (2016). Flowing with mindfulness: Investigating the relationship between flow and mindfulness. In I. Ivtzan & T. Lomas (Eds.), Mindfulness in positive psychology: The science of meditation and wellbeing (p. 141–155). Routledge/Taylor & Francis Group.

172 | Dixon, M., Gutierrez, J., Stange, M., Larche, C., Graydon, C., Vintan, S., & Kruger, T. (2019). Mindfulness Problems and Depression Symptoms in Everyday Life Predict Dark Flow During Slots Play: Implications for Gambling as a Form of Escape. Psychology of Addictive Behaviors, 33(1), 81-90.

173 | Neal, A., Ballard, T., & Vancouver, J. (2017). Dynamic Self-Regulation and Multiple-Goal Pursuit. Annual Review of Organizational Psychology and Organizational Behavior, 4, 401-423.

174 | Sperry, S., Knox, B., Edwards, D., Friedman, A., Rodriguez, M., Kaly, P., Albers, M., & Shaffer-Hudkins, E. (2014). Cultivating Healthy Eating, Exercise, and Relaxation (CHEER). Clinical Case Studies, 13(3), 218-230.

Ingvarsson, T., Nordén, T., Norlander, T. (2014) Mindfulness-Based Cognitive Therapy: A Case Study on Experiences of Healthy Behaviors by Clients in Psychiatric Care. Open Journal of Medical Psychology

Papies, E., Pronk, T., Keesman, M., & Barsalou, L. (2015). The Benefits of Simply Observing: Mindful Attention Modulates the Link Between Motivation and Behavior. Journal of Personality and Social Psychology, 108(1), 148-170.

175 | Segal, Z.V, Williams, J.M.G, Teasdale, J.D., (2013). Mindfulness-Based Cognitive Therapy for Depression, Second Edition: A New Approach to Preventing Relapse. The Guilford Press. New York, NY.

176 | DeMauro, A., Jennings, P., Cunningham, T., Fontaine, D., Park, H., & Sheras, P. (2019). Mindfulness and Caring in Professional Practice: an Interdisciplinary Review of Qualitative Research. Mindfulness, 10(10), 1969-1984.

Adair, K., Boulton, A., & Algoe, S. (2017). The Effect of Mindfulness on Relationship Satisfaction via Perceived Responsiveness: Findings from a Dyadic Study of Heterosexual Romantic Partners. Mindfulness, 9(2), 597-609.

177 | Edwards, M., (2020). The road beyond McMindfulness: What can we learn from 22 articles on mindfulness and social change? openDemocracy. Retrieved from: https://www.opendemocracy.net/en/transformation/road-beyond-mcmindfulness/

178 | Berry, D., Hoerr, J., Cesko, S., Alayoubi, A., Carpio, K., Zirzow, H., Walters, W., Scram, G., Rodriguez, K., & Beaver, V. (2020). Does Mindfulness Training Without Explicit Ethics-Based Instruction Promote Prosocial Behaviors? A Meta-Analysis. Personality and Social Psychology Bulletin, 1

179   Berry, D., Cairo, A., Goodman, R., Quaglia, J., Green, J., & Brown, K. (2018). Mindfulness Increases Prosocial Responses Toward Ostracized Strangers Through Empathic Concern. Journal of Experimental Psychology: General, 147(1), 93-112.}

Condon, P., Desbordes, G., Miller, W., & DeSteno, D. (2013). Meditation Increases Compassionate Responses to Suffering. Psychological Science, 24(10), 2125-2127; Lim, D., Condon, P., & DeSteno, D. (2015). Mindfulness and Compassion: An Examination of Mechanism and Scalability. PLoS ONE, 10(2),

180   Berry, D., Hoerr, J., Cesko, S., Alayoubi, A., Carpio, K., Zirzow, H., Walters, W., Scram, G., Rodriguez, K., & Beaver, V. (2020). Does Mindfulness Training Without Explicit Ethics-Based Instruction Promote Prosocial Behaviors? A Meta-Analysis. Personality and Social Psychology Bulletin, 1

181   Condon, P. (2017). Mindfulness, compassion, and prosocial behaviour. In J. C. Karremans & E. K. Papies (Eds.), Mindfulness in social psychology (p. 132)

182   Shapiro, S., (2012). Mindfulness-based stress reduction effects on moral reasoning and decision making. The journal of positive psychology. https://doi.org/10.1080/17439760.2012.723732

183   Ruedy, N., & Schweitzer, M. (2011). In the Moment: The Effect of Mindfulness on Ethical Decision Making. Journal of Business Ethics, 95(1), 73-87.;

184   Fischer, Daniel & Stanszus, Laura & Geiger, Sonja & Grossman, Paul & Schrader, Ulf. (2017). Mindfulness and Sustainable Consumption: A Systematic Literature Review of Research Approaches and Findings. Journal of Cleaner Production. 162. 544-558. 10.1016/j.jclepro.2017.06.007.

185   Sangvi, M., Bristow, J., Bell, R., (2019). Fieldbook for Mindfulness Innovators. The Mindfulness Initiative, Sheffield UK.

186   Baer, R. (2015). Ethics, Values, Virtues, and Character Strengths in Mindfulness-Based Interventions: a Psychological Science Perspective. Mindfulness, 6(4), 956-969.

187   Chen, S., & Jordan, C. (2020). Incorporating Ethics Into Brief Mindfulness Practice: Effects on Well-Being and Prosocial Behavior. Mindfulness, 11(1), 18-29.

188   Greenberg, M., & Mitra, J. (2015). From Mindfulness to Right Mindfulness: the Intersection of Awareness and Ethics. Mindfulness, 6(1), 74-78.

189   Schmidt, Andreas. (2016). The ethics and politics of mindfulness-based interventions. Journal of medical ethics. 42. 10.1136/medethics-2015-102942.

190   Hendersson, H., Wamsler, C., (2020). New stories for a more conscious, sustainable society: claiming authorship of the climate story. Climatic Change volume 158, pages345–359(2020)

Wamsler, C. (2018) Mind the gap: The role of mindfulness in adapting to increasing risk and climate change. Sustainability Science 13(4):1121–1135. Online.

191   Meadows, D., (1999). Leverage points: places to intervene in a system. The Sustainability Institute. Hartland, VT, USA.

192   Ives, C., Freeth, R., & Fischer, J. (2019). Inside-out sustainability: The neglect of inner worlds. Ambio, 49(1), 208-217.

Frank P., Fischer D., Wamsler C., (2020) 'Mindfulness, Education, and the Sustainable Development Goals', Leal Filho, W. et al. (Eds), book chapter in: Encyclopedia of the UN Sustainable Development Goals, Springer.

193   Keynote speech by Caroline Lucas MP delivered at the UK Mindfulness in Schools Conference 2019

194   Wamsler, C., Reeder, L., Crosweller, M. (2020) 'The being of urban resilience', Burayidi, M., Allen, A., Twigg, J., Wamsler, C. (Eds.), book chapter in: Handbook of Urban Resilience, , Routledge. Available here.

195   Fischer, Daniel & Stanszus, Laura & Geiger, Sonja & Grossman, Paul & Schrader, Ulf. (2017). Mindfulness and Sustainable Consumption: A Systematic Literature Review of Research Approaches and Findings. Journal of Cleaner Production. 162. 544-558. 10.1016/j.jclepro.2017.06.007.

196   Wamsler, C., Brossmann, J., Hendersson, H. et al. (2018). Mindfulness in sustainability science, practice, and teaching. Sustain Sci 13, 143–162. https://doi.org/10.1007/s11625-017-0428-2

Thiermann, U.B., Sheate, W.R. (2020). The Way Forward in Mindfulness and Sustainability: a Critical Review and Research Agenda. J Cogn Enhanc. https://doi.org/10.1007/s41465-020-00180-6

Wamsler, C., Brink, E. (2018) Mindsets for sustainability: Exploring the link between mindfulness and sustainable climate adaptation, Ecological Economics 151:55–61.

197   Bregman, R. (2020). Human kind: A Hopeful History. Bloomsbury Publishing. London, UK.

198   Kirby, J.N., Tellegen, C.L., Steindl, S.R., (2017). A Meta-Analysis of Compassion-Based Interventions: Current State of Knowledge and Future Directions. Behavior Therapy 48 (2017) 778–792.

199   Adnan, I. (2020). The Politics Of Waking Up 1: Power And Possibility In The Fractal Age. Retrieved from http://www.whatisemerging.com/opinions/the-politics-of-waking-up-power-and-possibility-in-the-fractal-age

200   Bihari, J., & Mullan, E. (2012). Relating Mindfully: A Qualitative Exploration of Changes in Relationships Through Mindfulness-Based Cognitive Therapy. Mindfulness, 5(1), 46-59.

201   Allen, M., Bromley, A., Kuyken, W., Sonnenberg, S J. (2009) Participants' Experiences of Mindfulness-Based Cognitive Therapy: "It Changed Me in Just about Every Way Possible". Behavioural and Cognitive Psychotherapy, 2009, 37, 413–430 - https://pdfs.semanticscholar.org/abbb/11872118947863526dfe7df138fa473795af.pdf

202   Bentley, P., Kaplan, S., & Mokonogho, J. (2018). Relational Mindfulness for Psychiatry Residents: a Pilot Course in Empathy Development and Burnout Prevention. Academic Psychiatry, 42(5), 668-673.

203   Rupprecht, S., Falke, P., Kohls, N., Tamdjidi, C., Wittmann, M., Kersemaekers, W. (2019). Mindful Leader Development: How Leaders Experience the Effects of Mindfulness Training on Leader Capabilities. Front Psychol. 2019;10:1081. doi:10.3389/fpsyg.2019.01081

Vreeling K, Kersemaekers W, Cillessen L, et al. How medical specialists experience the effects of a mindful leadership course on their leadership capabilities: a qualitative interview study in the Netherlands. BMJ Open 2019;9:e031643. doi:10.1136/ bmjopen-2019-031643

204   Karremans, J., van Schie, H., van Dongen, I., Kappen, G., Mori, G., van As, S., ten Bokkel, I., & van der Wal, R. (2019). Is Mindfulness Associated With Interpersonal Forgiveness?. Emotion, 1

205   Lueke, Adam & Gibson, Bryan. (2016). Brief Mindfulness Meditation Reduces Discrimination.. Psychology of Consciousness: Theory, Research, and Practice. 3. 10.1037/cns0000081.

206   Long, E., & Christian, M. (2015). Mindfulness Buffers Retaliatory Responses to Injustice: A Regulatory Approach. Journal of Applied Psychology, 100(5), 1409-1422.

207   Alkoby, A., Halperin, E., Tarrasch, R., & Levit-Binnun, N. (2017). Increased Support for Political Compromise in the Israeli-Palestinian Conflict Following an 8-Week Mindfulness Workshop. Mindfulness, 8(5), 1345-1353.; Leonard L. Riskin, Mindfulness: Foundational Training for Dispute Resolution, 54 J. Legal Educ. 79 (2004), available at http://scholarship.law.ufl.edu/facultypub/636

208   Callister, R., Geddes, D., & Gibson, D. (2017). When Is Anger Helpful or Hurtful? Status and Role Impact on Anger Expression and Outcomes. Negotiation and Conflict Management Research, 10(2), 69-87.

209   Bommarito, N., (2017). Virtuous And Vicious Anger. Journal Of Ethics & Social Philosophy | Vol. 11, No. 3

210   Bowlin, N.A, & Beehr, T.A. (2006) Workplace harassment from the vicitim's perspective: a theoretical model and meta-analysis. Journal of Applied Psychology, 91: 998-1012.

211   Callister, R., Geddes, D., & Gibson, D. (2017). When Is Anger Helpful or Hurtful? Status and Role Impact on Anger Expression and Outcomes. Negotiation and Conflict Management Research, 10(2), 69-87.

212   Eisenlohr-Moul, T., Peters, J., Pond, R., & DeWall, C. (2016). Both Trait and State Mindfulness Predict Lower Aggressiveness via Anger Rumination: a Multilevel Mediation Analysis. Mindfulness, 7(3), 713-726.

213 | Stephens, A.N., Koppel, S., Young, K. L., Chambers, R., Hassed, C. (2018) Associations between self-reported mindfulness, driving anger and aggressive driving. Transportation Research Part F: Traffic Psychology and Behaviour. 56:149-155.

214 | Krishnakumar, S., & Robinson, M. (2015). Maintaining An Even Keel: An Affect-Mediated Model of Mindfulness and Hostile Work Behavior. Emotion, 15(5), 579-589.

215 | Eisenlohr-Moul, T., Peters, J., Pond, R., & DeWall, C. (2016). Both Trait and State Mindfulness Predict Lower Aggressiveness via Anger Rumination: a Multilevel Mediation Analysis. Mindfulness, 7(3), 713-726.

216 | Liang, L., Brown, D., Ferris, D., Hanig, S., Lian, H., & Keeping, L. (2018). The Dimensions and Mechanisms of Mindfulness in Regulating Aggressive Behaviors. Journal of Applied Psychology, 103(3), 281-299.

217 | Wachs, K., & Cordova, J. (2007). Mindful Relating: Exploring Mindfulness and Emotion Repertoires in Intimate Relationships. Journal of Marital and Family Therapy, 33(4),

218 | Bögels, S M. Emerson, L-M. (2019). The mindful family: a systemic approach to mindfulness, relational functioning, and somatic and mental health. Current Opinion in Psychology. 28:138-142. https://doi.org/10.1016/j.copsyc.2018.12.001

219 | Abdollah Omidi, A., Raygan, F., Akbari, H., Momeni, J. The effects of mindfulness-based stress reduction on cardiac patients' blood pressure, perceived stress, and anger: a single-blind randomized controlled trial

220 | Singh, N. N., Lancioni, G. E., Karazsia, B. T., Winton, A. S., Singh, J., & Wahler, R. G. (2014). Shenpa and compassionate abiding: mindfulness-based practices for anger and aggression by individuals with schizophrenia. International Journal of Mental Health and Addiction, 12(2), 138–152.

221 | Ahemaitijiang, N., Hu, X., Yang, X., & Han, Z. (2020). Effects of Meditation on the Soles of the Feet on the Aggressive and Destructive Behaviors of Chinese Adolescents with Autism Spectrum Disorders. Mindfulness, 11(1), 230-240.

222 | Singh, N.N., & Hwang, .Y. (2020). Mindfulness-based programs and practices for people with intellectual and developmental disability. Current Opinion in Psychiatry, 33(2),

223 | Rodriguez Vega, B., Melero-Llorente, J., Bayon Perez, C., Cebolla, S., Mira, J., Valverde, C., & Fernández-Liria, A. (2014). Impact of mindfulness training on attentional control and anger regulation processes for psychotherapists in training. Psychotherapy Research, 24(2), 202–213.

224 | Bergman, A., Christopher, M., & Bowen, S. (2016). Changes in Facets of Mindfulness Predict Stress and Anger Outcomes for Police Officers. Mindfulness, 7(4), 851-858.

225 | Per, M., Spinelli, C., Sadowski, I., Schmelefske, E., Anand, L., & Khoury, B. (2020). Evaluating the Effectiveness of Mindfulness-Based Interventions in Incarcerated Populations: A Meta-Analysis. Criminal Justice and Behavior, 47(3), 310-330.

226 | Batson 2010; de Waal 2008; Eisenberg 2000; Haidt 2003b; Hoffman 1975; Tangney et al. 2007, Davis & Oathout 1987.

227 | Luberto, C., Shinday, N., Song, R., Philpotts, L., Park, E., Fricchione, G., & Yeh, G. (2017). A Systematic Review and Meta-analysis of the Effects of Meditation on Empathy, Compassion, and Prosocial Behaviors. Mindfulness, 9(3), 708-724.

228 | James N. Donald, J., Sahdra, B., Van Zanden2, B., Duineveld, J., Atkins, P., Marshall, S., Ciarrochi, J. (2019). Does your mindfulness benefit others? A systematic review and meta-analysis of the link between mindfulness and prosocial behaviour. British Journal of Psychology (2019), 110, 101–125.

229 | Laneri, D., Krach, S., Paulus, F., Kanske, P., Schuster, V., Sommer, J., & Müller-Pinzler, L. (2017). Mindfulness meditation regulates anterior insula activity during empathy for social pain. Human Brain Mapping, 38(8), 4034-4046.

230   Tirch, D. (2010). Mindfulness as a Context for the Cultivation of Compassion. International Journal of Cognitive Therapy, 3(2), 113-123.

Hildebrandt, L., McCall, C., & Singer, T. (2017). Differential Effects of Attention-, Compassion-, and Socio-Cognitively Based Mental Practices on Self-Reports of Mindfulness and Compassion. Mindfulness, 8(6), 1488-1512.

231   Trautweina, F-M. Kanskebe, P. Böcklerc, A. Singer, T. (2020). Differential benefits of mental training types for attention, compassion, and theory of mind. Cognition. https://doi.org/10.1016/j.cognition.2019.104039

232   Bartels-Velthuis, A., Schroevers, M., van der Ploeg, K., Koster, F., Fleer, J., & van den Brink, E. (2016). A Mindfulness-Based Compassionate Living Training in a Heterogeneous Sample of Psychiatric Outpatients: a Feasibility Study. Mindfulness, 7, 809-818.

233   Paul Gilbert (2010). An Introduction to Compassion Focused Therapy in Cognitive Behavior Therapy. International Journal of Cognitive Therapy: Vol. 3, Special Section: Compassion Focused Therapy, pp. 97-112. https://doi.org/10.1521/ijct.2010.3.2.97.

234   Neff, K., & Germer, C. (2013). A Pilot Study and Randomized Controlled Trial of the Mindful Self-Compassion Program. Journal of Clinical Psychology, 69(1), 28-44.

235   Neff, K., Germer, C. (2018). The Mindful Self-Compassion Workbook: A Proven Way to Accept Yourself, Build Inner Strength, and Thrive. The Guilford Press, New York, London.

236   Singer, P. (1981). Expanding Circle.

237   Pinker, S., (2011). The Better Angels of Our Nature: Why Violence Has Declined. Penguin. London, UK

238   Dorje, OT. (2017) Interconnected: Embracing Life in Our Global Society. Wisdom. Somerville, MA, USA.

239   UK Mindfulness All-Party Parliamentary Group (2015). Mindful Nation UK. The Mindfulness Initiative. https://www.themindfulnessinitiative.org/mindful-nation-report

240   Bristow, J. (2017). How Mindfulness will Protect You From Being Replaced by a Robot. Mindful Online. Retrieved from: https://www.mindful.org/can-mindfulness-help-us-navigate-fourth-industrial-revolution/

McDonald, T., (2019). Humanics: A way to 'robot-proof' your career? BBC. Retrieved from: https://www.bbc.com/worklife/article/20190127-humanics-a-way-to-robot-proof-your-career

Milton Keynes UK
Ingram Content Group UK Ltd.
UKHW051602010224
437102UK00013B/178